Editor
Nancy Hoffman

Managing Editor
Karen J. Goldfluss, M.S. Ed.

Illustrator
Sue Fullam

Cover Artist
Brenda DiAntonis

Art Manager
Kevin Barnes

Art Director
CJae Froshay

Imaging
Alfred Lau
James Edward Grace

Publisher
Mary D. Smith, M.S. Ed.

Spotlight On AMERICA

Grades 4–8

Colonial America

Author

Robert W. Smith

Teacher Created Resources

Teacher Created Resources, Inc.
6421 Industry Way
Westminster, CA 92683
www.teachercreated.com

ISBN-1-4206-3213-2

©2005 Teacher Created Resources, Inc.
Reprinted, 2006
Made in U.S.A.

Table of Contents

Introduction

The *Spotlight on America* series is designed to introduce some of the seminal events in American history to students in the fourth through eighth grades. Reading in the content area is enriched with a balanced variety of activities in written language, social studies, science, and oral expression. The series is designed to make history literally come alive in your classroom and take root in the minds of your students.

The colonial era was a period of critical importance in forming the nation we have become. The attitudes toward personal liberty, freedom of religion, and equal opportunity which gradually evolved have helped to form the conscience of the nation throughout its history. The demands for political equality, religious liberty, personal opportunity, and land ownership grew with the nation and transformed it from a few colonies along the Atlantic coast to a nation that stretched across the continent. The influx of immigrants from many lands helped fuel a constantly changing economy. Although the colonial settlers retained a foundation of British laws, language, and culture, they created a nation to meet the challenges of a diverse population living in a rugged and dangerous new land.

A fascinating collection of characters exemplified the colonial era, and few are well known to the general public today. People as different as John Smith and Eliza Lucas Pinckney, John Winthrop and Anne Hutchinson, and Metacom and Olaudah Equiano created a nation diverse in thought but fueled by enormous personal passion and energy. The nation they helped create has endured and flourished despite world wars, economic depressions, civil war, riots, and other major crises.

The reading selections and comprehension questions in this book serve to introduce the colonial era. They also set the stage for activities in other subject areas. The writing and oral language activities are designed to help students sense the drama and danger that surrounded life on the edge of civilization. Students should sense the urgency of events and the cultural milieu of the times when doing the research activities. These are intended to make students aware of the events and leaders who lived during the colonial centuries. The aim of the culminating activities is to acquaint students with the life and times of people in the new settlements.

Enjoy using this book with your students, and look for other books in this series.

1600   1650   1700   1750   1800   1850

Teacher Lesson Plans for Reading Comprehension

Founding the Colonies 1607–1636

Objective: Students will demonstrate fluency and comprehension in reading historically based text.

Materials: copies of Founding the Colonies 1607–1636 (pages 8–10); copies of Founding the Colonies 1607–1636 Quiz (page 33); additional reading selections from books, encyclopedias, and Internet sources for enrichment

Procedure

1. Reproduce and distribute Founding the Colonies 1607–1636 (pages 8–10). Review pre-reading skills by briefly reviewing text and encouraging students to underline, make marginal notes, list questions, and highlight unfamiliar words as they read.

2. Assign the reading as classwork or homework.

3. As a class, discuss the following questions or others of your choosing.

   • Which colony was in the greatest danger of failing? Why?

   • In which colony would you have preferred to be a settler? Why?

   • Which colony treated everyone most fairly? How so?

Assessment: Have students complete the Founding the Colonies 1607–1636 Quiz (page 33). Correct the quiz together.

Founding the Colonies 1636–1733

Objective: Students will demonstrate fluency and comprehension in reading historically based text.

Materials: copies of Founding the Colonies 1636–1733 (pages 11–13); copies of Founding the Colonies 1636–1733 Quiz (page 34); additional reading selections from books, encyclopedias, and Internet sources for enrichment

Procedure

1. Reproduce and distribute Founding the Colonies 1636–1733 (pages 11–13). Review pre-reading skills by briefly reviewing text and encouraging students to underline, make marginal notes, list questions, and highlight unfamiliar words as they read.

2. Assign the reading as classwork or homework.

3. As a class, discuss the following questions or others of your choosing.

   • Which colony seemed the most successful? Why?

   • In your opinion, which founder of a colony received the best gift from the king? Why?

   • Which colony would be best to live in if you were poor? A Native American? An African American?

Assessment: Have students complete the Founding the Colonies 1636–1733 Quiz (page 34). Correct the quiz together.

Teacher Lesson Plans for Reading Comprehension *(cont.)*

Colonial Lifestyles

Objective: Students will demonstrate fluency and comprehension in reading historically based text.

Materials: copies of Colonial Lifestyles (pages 14–16); copies of Colonial Lifestyles Quiz (page 35); additional reading selections from books, encyclopedias, and Internet sources for enrichment

Procedure

1. Reproduce and distribute Colonial Lifestyles (pages 14–16). Review pre-reading skills by briefly reviewing text and encouraging students to underline, make marginal notes, list questions, and highlight unfamiliar words as they read.

2. Assign the reading as classwork or homework.

3. As a class, discuss the following questions or others of your choosing.

   • Which form of colonial punishment seemed the most severe? Why?

   • How would you travel if you lived in colonial times?

   • What aspect of colonial life would you find the most uncomfortable?

Assessment: Have students complete the Colonial Lifestyles Quiz (page 35). Correct the quiz together.

Children and Education

Objective: Students will demonstrate fluency and comprehension in reading historically based text.

Materials: copies of Children and Education (pages 17–19); copies of Children and Education Quiz (page 36); additional reading selections from books, encyclopedias, and Internet sources for enrichment

Procedure

1. Reproduce and distribute Children and Education (pages 17–19). Review pre-reading skills by briefly reviewing text and encouraging students to underline, make marginal notes, list questions, and highlight unfamiliar words as they read.

2. Assign the reading as classwork or homework.

3. As a class, discuss the following questions or others of your choosing.

   • How is table behavior different today for children than it was in colonial days?

   • What are some of the differences between schools in colonial times and today?

   • Do you think you would have liked being an apprentice? Why?

Assessment: Have students complete the Children and Education Quiz (page 36). Correct the quiz together.

Teacher Lesson Plans for Reading Comprehension *(cont.)*

Native Americans and New Settlers

Objective: Students will demonstrate fluency and comprehension in reading historically based text.

Materials: copies of Native Americans and New Settlers (pages 20–23); copies of Native Americans and New Settlers Quiz (page 37); additional reading selections from books, encyclopedias, and Internet sources for enrichment

Procedure

1. Reproduce and distribute Native Americans and New Settlers (pages 20–23). Review pre-reading skills by briefly reviewing text and encouraging students to underline, make marginal notes, list questions, and highlight unfamiliar words as they read.

2. Assign the reading as classwork or homework.

3. As a class, discuss the following questions or others of your choosing.

   • How were Indians affected by the white settlements?

   • What might have happened if all settlers had been like William Penn and Roger Williams?

   • Why was trade so important to both Native Americans and new settlers?

Assessment: Have students complete the Native Americans and New Settlers Quiz (page 37). Correct the quiz together.

Indentured Servitude and Slavery

Objective: Students will demonstrate fluency and comprehension in reading historically based text.

Materials: copies of Indentured Servitude and Slavery (pages 24–27); copies of Indentured Servitude and Slavery Quiz (page 38); additional reading selections from books, encyclopedias, and Internet sources for enrichment

Procedure

1. Reproduce and distribute Indentured Servitude and Slavery (pages 24–27). Review pre-reading skills by briefly reviewing text and encouraging students to underline, make marginal notes, list questions, and highlight unfamiliar words as they read.

2. Assign the reading as classwork or homework.

3. As a class, discuss the following questions or others of your choosing.

   • What were some of the advantages and disadvantages of being an indentured servant?

   • What was the worst aspect of life as a slave? Why?

   • How do you think slaves found the strength to survive?

Assessment: Have students complete the Indentured Servitude and Slavery Quiz (page 38). Correct the quiz together.

Teacher Lesson Plans for Reading Comprehension *(cont.)*

Colonial Leaders

Objective: Students will demonstrate fluency and comprehension in reading historically based text.

Materials: copies of Colonial Leaders (pages 28–32); copies of Colonial Leaders Quiz (page 39); additional reading selections from books, encyclopedias, and Internet sources for enrichment

Procedure

1. Reproduce and distribute Colonial Leaders (pages 28–32). Review pre-reading skills by briefly reviewing text and encouraging students to underline, make marginal notes, list questions, and highlight unfamiliar words as they read.

2. Assign the reading as classwork or homework.

3. As a class, discuss the following questions or others of your choosing.

   • Which colonial leader do you think had the most interesting life?

   • Which leader would you like to have known? Why?

   • Which leader was the most important to his settlement or followers? Why?

Assessment: Have students complete the Colonial Leaders Quiz (page 39). Correct the quiz together.

Founding the Colonies 1607–1636

Virginia (Founded in 1607)

The first permanent English settlement was founded at Jamestown, Virginia. More than half of the men were gentlemen who were looking for fortune and adventure and were untrained in any work. Eight thousand of the first 10,000 settlers at Jamestown died during the first few years. Starvation and disease killed most of them, but Indian attacks and accidents also took their toll.

The colony would probably have failed had it not been led by John Smith, a shrewd and stubborn leader. He required every person to work who wanted to eat, including those gentlemen who were not used to hard labor. Smith kept an uneasy peace with the local natives and also mapped much of the area. In 1619 landowners elected representatives called *Burgesses* to help the royal governor make laws. This was the first representative assembly in America.

Massachusetts (Founded in 1620)

Puritans were religious dissenters who wanted to purify and change the Church of England. In 1620 about 40 Pilgrims boarded the ship *Mayflower* to travel to the New World. They got off course and landed at Plymouth in November 1620. Before they landed, 41 men signed a compact to form a government for the community, and they also elected a governor.

Over the harsh winter, half of these original settlers succumbed to hunger and disease. The next spring a local Indian named Squanto taught them how to raise crops, and in the fall of 1621, they celebrated a Thanksgiving feast with the neighboring Indians in gratitude for their survival.

The Massachusetts Bay Colony was established in 1630 by a thousand Pilgrims who settled up the coast from Plymouth. They founded the city of Boston, and other villages rapidly developed because the Massachusetts Bay Company offered free land to settlers.

1600   1650   1700   1750   1800   1850

Founding the Colonies 1607–1636 *(cont.)*

New Hampshire (Founded in 1623)

Captain John Smith first claimed the area of New Hampshire for England in 1614 while mapping New England. In 1622 King James gave this land to John Mason and Sir Ferdinando Gorges. In 1623 David Thomson and 20 English settlers built Pannaway Plantation, the first European settlement in New Hampshire. In 1629 Mason and Gorges divided the land they had been given. Gorges took the area that would eventually become Maine, and Mason received New Hampshire. Although Mason never came to America, he did send settlers. The new settlers grew corn, beans, and pumpkins and raised sheep, cattle, and pigs. They fished along the coast, trapped beavers, and cut down trees to use for building British ships.

New York (Founded in 1624)

The Dutch claimed the area originally explored by Henry Hudson and called it New Netherland. In 1624 the Dutch West India Company sent 18 families to create a settlement near what is now Albany, New York. The following year Dutch settlers founded New Amsterdam on the island of Manhattan. In 1626 Peter Minuet, the governor of the colony, bought Manhattan Island from the Indians in exchange for knives, beads, and cloth estimated at a value of about $24 in modern currency.

The colony grew rapidly and welcomed people from many countries and religious persuasions. In 1647 Peter Stuyvesant, who wore a wooden leg, became governor of New Netherland. He made the city of New Amsterdam safer and organized the first police department, regular garbage collection, a post office, and a hospital. In 1664 King Charles II of England sent his brother James and a fleet to take New Netherland from the Dutch. The English renamed it New York, in honor of James, the Duke of York. In 1691 New York became a royal colony ruled by the king of England.

Connecticut (Founded in 1633)

The first European to explore Connecticut was the Dutch explorer Adriaen Black, who gave it the Indian name *Quinnenhtukqut*, which was later changed to Connecticut. Thomas Hooker, a Puritan religious exile from England, came to Massachusetts from Holland. Conflicts with leaders in Massachusetts caused him to lead 100 settlers to Hartford. Thousands followed, and three towns on the Connecticut River—Windsor, Hartford, and Wethersfield—united to become the Connecticut colony. In 1639 Hooker wrote his ideas of religious and civic freedom as the Fundamental Orders, and these were the basis of Connecticut law until 1662.

Founding the Colonies 1607–1636 *(cont.)*

Maryland (Founded in 1634)

In 1632 King Charles I gave Sir George Calvert and his family a charter to start a colony north of Virginia as a haven for Catholics. The colony was called Maryland in honor of the king's wife, Henrietta Maria. George's son Leonard Calvert and 200 colonists landed in Maryland in 1634. They bought land from the Indians and named their first settlement St. Mary's. About 25 of the original colonists had paid their way to the colony and were given land. These wealthy families then brought other people to Maryland as *bondservants*, who had to work for the plantation owner for seven years before they earned their freedom.

Disease and hunger caused many deaths in the early years, and almost every child lost at least one parent. Leonard Calvert had to return to England from 1644 to 1646, and the colony went through two years of disorder, widespread plundering, and religious feuding between Protestants and Catholics. In 1649 Maryland's lawmakers passed the Act of Toleration, which allowed Christian religious groups to practice their religion and to own land.

Rhode Island (Founded in 1636)

Roger Williams, a Puritan leader in Massachusetts, believed people should have the right to express their opinions about religion whether or not the Puritan elders agreed. He also criticized the taking of Indian lands. By 1636 Williams had so aggravated the leaders of Massachusetts that they planned to arrest him and deport him to England. He left the colony and went to Narraganset Bay, where he spent months with friendly Wampanoag Indians.

Williams wanted to create a colony where the government would be separate from the church. In 1636 Williams and some followers bought land from the Indians and founded the city of Providence. Disgruntled refugees from Massachusetts also built three other neighboring cities. In 1643 the four towns banded together and officially became a colony. The king gave Roger Williams a charter allowing Rhode Island full independence from other colonies. A new charter in 1663 gave full religious freedom to all. The charter also gave them the freedom to elect their own representatives and governor.

Founding the Colonies 1636–1733

Delaware (Founded in 1638)

The English explorer and navigator Henry Hudson first explored Delaware Bay in 1609. In 1610 English sea captain Samuel Argall was caught in a storm in the same bay and named it in honor of Lord de la Warr, the governor of Virginia. The Dutch began a settlement in Delaware in 1631 that was completely wiped out in an accidental conflict with neighboring Indians of the Lenape tribe. In 1637 Peter Minuet brought Swedish settlers to Delaware and started a settlement called New Sweden in what is now Wilmington. They paid for the land, build a fort, and also built the first log houses in colonial America, modeled on homes in Sweden.

In 1651 the Dutch built a fort near the Swedish settlement, and the two nations fought over Delaware with settlements captured and recaptured until 1664 when England became involved in the conflict. The brother of the British king took several ships and 300 soldiers and defeated the Dutch in 1664. Delaware then became an English royal colony.

Pennsylvania (Founded in 1643)

In 1643 Swedish colonists created a settlement called New Sweden on Tinicum Island near what is today Philadelphia. Dutch soldiers captured the settlement in 1655 and controlled it for nine years. Then in 1664 the brother of King Charles of England took control of the area. In 1681 King Charles II gave the land—28 million acres—to his friend William Penn to whom he owed a great deal of money. Penn named the colony Pennsylvania, meaning "Penn's Woods."

As a Quaker, William Penn believed in peace and equality. He wanted to establish a colony as a haven for his people, who were often harassed and arrested in England for practicing their beliefs. In 1682 William Penn sailed for America along with 100 Quakers. The city he created was called Philadelphia, meaning "City of Brotherly Love" in Greek.

Penn created a Frame of Government, which allowed people to be tried by jury and all landowners to vote. In addition, Christian believers could worship in any form they wished. Penn also made peace with the Indians. Slavery was discouraged, although some people did own slaves. Pennsylvania became one of the leading colonies in America with more than 4,000 settlers by 1700 and successful farms, businesses, and trading companies.

Founding the Colonies 1636–1733 *(cont.)*

North Carolina (Founded in 1653)

The first attempted settlement in what is now North Carolina was founded in 1587 by sea captains under the command of Sir Walter Raleigh. That settlement on Roanoke Island vanished within three years, and no one knows what happened to its settlers. North Carolina was considered a part of Virginia until 1629 when Virginia was divided into Virginia and Carolana ("land of Charles," named after King Charles). Settlers from Virginia looking for good land and freedom of religion settled in this area.

In 1663 King Charles gave Carolana to eight friends called *lords proprietors*, who renamed the area Carolina. These absentee owners charged rents to colonists who had settled in the area. Some farmers revolted against the rents in 1677, and they imprisoned the governor and ran the colony themselves for two years. In 1712 Carolina was divided into two parts, and in 1729 King George the III bought back North Carolina from the proprietors.

New Jersey (Founded in 1660)

Henry Hudson explored the coast of New Jersey in 1609, giving the Dutch government a claim to the area. In 1624 the Dutch built Fort Nassau on the Delaware River. In 1643 the Swedes built Fort Elfsborg near the Dutch fort. In 1655 Dutch leader Peter Stuyvesant marched to the Swedish fort and demanded its surrender. The Swedes surrendered without a fight.

In 1664 English ships and soldiers under the command of James, the brother of the king of England, captured New Netherlands, which included what is now New Jersey. James gave this land to two friends, Sir George Carteret and Lord John Berkeley, and renamed the area New Jersey because Carteret was from the British Isle of Jersey. The two men were proprietors who charged rents to settlers living on their land. They offered cheap land and freedom of religion to encourage settlement, but they were poor leaders. In 1674 Lord Berkeley sold his land to two Quakers, who called the area West Jersey. Carteret's widow later sold East Jersey to 24 men. Neither Jersey was very prosperous, and in 1702 East and West Jersey joined together again and became a royal colony ruled by the king of England.

Founding the Colonies 1636–1733 *(cont.)*

South Carolina (Founded in 1670)

Both Spain and France attempted to establish settlements in South Carolina in the late 1500s, but neither was successful. King Charles named the land *Carolana* after himself in 1629 when it was separated from Virginia. In 1663 his son Charles II renamed it Carolina and gave the land to eight noblemen called lords proprietors, who had helped him regain the English throne. In 1669 these absentee owners sent 100 settlers, who survived storms and two shipwrecks, to start a settlement which became known as Charles Town (now Charleston). They were the first settlers to plan where streets would go before building the town. Although it was difficult to grow food, land was cheap and people of diverse religious beliefs were welcome. In 1712 the two Carolinas became separate colonies.

Over time the settlers became enraged at the absentee proprietors, who sent governors to collect rents and rule the colony. The governors often cheated the settlers, raised the rents, and failed to protect them from Indian attacks. In 1719 the colonists revolted and threw the governor out of office. They asked King George for permission to become a royal colony, and he agreed.

Georgia (Founded in 1733)

James Oglethorpe, a visionary leader, decided to start a colony in the New World as a haven for *debtors*, people who were put in jail because they owed money and could not repay their debts. Oglethorpe named the colony Georgia in honor of King George II, who gave him a royal charter in 1732 to establish the colony. In 1733 Oglethorpe led 114 colonists—including debtors, adventurers, and others seeking a better life—to a bluff overlooking a river. He called the city Savannah and carefully laid out a plan for city growth.

Oglethorpe hoped to make Georgia a *utopia*, a perfect place to live. He established laws forbidding the buying and selling of liquor because he felt drinking made people lazy and belligerent. Slavery was forbidden because Oglethorpe was opposed to the idea of people owning other people. However, in 1750 Georgians changed the laws so that slavery became legal and liquor could be sold. In 1752 Georgia became a royal colony.

Colonial Lifestyles

The New England Colonies

Most settlers in the New England colonies did some farming, but the land was actually poor for growing crops. It was strewn with rocks and tree stumps, and the growing season was short. There were many fine harbors, however, and many colonists were involved in fishing, shipbuilding, and shipping goods to and from other colonies and England. There were many merchants, artisans, and skilled workers in these towns. Most families lived near a village, shopped regularly, and attended weekly church services. Many of the citizens were Puritans or other dissenters from the official Church of England. The New England colonies included Massachusetts, Connecticut, Rhode Island, and New Hampshire.

The Middle Colonies

New York, Delaware, New Jersey, and Pennsylvania comprised the middle colonies. There were many English settlers but also people from Germany, Sweden, Scotland, the Netherlands, and other countries. These colonies were often freer about practicing unpopular religions and were open to Quakers, Catholics, Jews, and dissenters from established churches in Europe. Most people owned small farms, although some wealthy landowners had huge holdings, especially in New York and New Jersey. The most powerful Indian tribe was the Iroquois, a powerful confederation of tribes in New York.

The Southern Colonies

Agriculture dominated the economy of the southern colonies. Large plantations were established by successful landowners and used to grow cash crops, which were exported rather than sold to the local population. Tobacco, rice, wheat, and *indigo* (a blue dye) were the main cash crops. This kind of economy required a large supply of cheap labor. Although indentured servants were used in the early years of settlement, the importation of black slaves from Africa soon became the source of cheap labor. The southern colonies included Virginia, Maryland, Georgia, North Carolina, and South Carolina. Charleston, South Carolina, and Savannah, Georgia, were thriving ports where crops could be exported and supplies imported.

Colonial Lifestyles *(cont.)*

Travel and Transportation

The fastest way to travel anywhere during colonial times was by water. Colonists crossed the Atlantic Ocean in sailing ships to get to the New World. Most early towns and cities were built along the Atlantic coast or near rivers so that trade and travel would be easier. Rafts, keelboats, and canoes were used to travel along rivers and streams. Cities such as Boston, New York, Philadelphia, Baltimore, and Charleston developed into important ports.

On land most people traveled by foot. Some colonists could walk as many as 30 miles in 10 hours. Roads were usually trails or dirt tracks used by wagons. Some rode horses, and many families owned a wagon. A few wealthy men owned carriages or coaches. People traveling from one city to another on business usually took a stagecoach, which provided a bone-jarring ride, often punctuated by bad weather, impassable roads, mechanical breakdowns, and the sheer monotony of a long, dusty ride. By the mid-1700s there was a network of roads connecting the major cities.

Village Life

Village life during colonial times would shock most modern Americans. The streets were rarely paved. They were muddy in the wet seasons and full of dirt at all times. Waste products from horses, cattle, and free-roaming pigs ended up in the streets. It was noisy, too, with the sounds of people and animals, rattling carts, and the hammering of craftsmen.

Strangers were usually distrusted. The sheriff might warn a stranger that if he caused any trouble he would be run out of town or arrested. Because many con men and other criminals were travelers, this was sometimes a sensible precaution. People were very impressed by family connections, titles, wealth, length of residence in a community, education, and political influence.

Personal Hygiene

It is difficult today to imagine the sanitary conditions that were common during colonial times. The only showers that people took occurred when they were caught in a thunderstorm, and baths were virtually unknown. Sometimes men and boys took a swim in the summer, but women and girls rarely bathed. Deodorant had not come into use, and perfume was seldom used. Clothes were washed only about once a month and sometimes even less often. Many colonists had pockmarks on their faces from having contracted and survived smallpox.

Colonial Lifestyles (cont.)

Crime and Punishment

In colonial days, punishments for criminal offenses involved both shame and physical pain. In fact, almost all punishments involved some form of public humiliation witnessed by the community and family. By today's standards, they seem exceedingly degrading.

Stocks were wooden frameworks in which the ankles and wrists were locked while the criminal sat on the ground. These could be used for people who were public nuisances and also for more serious crimes. The *pillory* was a favorite punishment for treason, witchcraft, perjury, wife beating, forgery, cheating, fortune telling, or drunkenness. The pillory had holes for the victim's head and hands. People were permitted to throw stones or rotten food at the person in the pillory. A *bilboe* was a long heavy bar used to shackle and hold a culprit up by the legs.

Criminals could also be tied to the whipping post and publicly flogged for everything from disturbing the peace to being a slave running away from an owner. The *ducking stool* was another method used. It had a seat tied to a long rail. The person sentenced to this form of punishment was ducked in and out of a pond or river several times. It was a popular punishment for scolds, nagging women, and quarrelsome couples.

Gossips and nagging women often were forced to wear a *gossip's bridle*, or *brank*. It was an iron cage over the head with an iron tongue, often with spikes, placed over the victim's tongue. Poor communities made do with a split shaft of wood placed over the tongue. Neither afforded the gossip any opportunity to talk.

Criminals often had their ears sliced partially or completely off or were branded. A person branded with a capital "T" was a thief. A criminal could wear an "F" for forgery, a "B" for burglar, or an "R" for rogue or vagabond. Capital crimes, which carried the death penalty, were usually carried out on the gallows where men were hanged and their bodies sometimes allowed to rot as a warning to other criminals.

16

Children and Education

Children and Chores

Although children enjoyed playing and adults valued opportunities to recreate, every member of the family and the colonial community worked long hours. Even small children barely past the toddler stage were expected to work. Children arose at dawn with the rest of the family. They gathered firewood, shucked corn, made their beds, and did errands.

Older children often attended school when they were not needed to work in the fields. But before and after school and during days off, they fed the animals, milked cows, worked in the garden, cut wood, made brooms, churned butter, made candles and soap, and often helped prepare meals or clean up afterward. Many children learned to hunt alone for squirrels, possums, rabbits, and other small animals before they were 10 years old.

Games and Entertainment

When they were not doing chores, children enjoyed many simple games and activities. They liked walking on stilts, rolling hoops, or playing with tops. They played Blindman's Bluff and hide-and-seek. Children made and flew kites and went fishing in nearby brooks. They also had swings on trees and seesaw boards. They bowled on grass or dirt, rolled marbles, and played *quoits* by trying to toss a ring over a stake. Some colonists also enjoyed playing board games, charades, card games, and chess in the evening. A few had time to read or play a musical instrument, such as the violin.

At the Table

Children often did not sit at the main table with their parents. In some cases, they stood behind an adult who handed them food. In other homes, they sat at a separate table or at one end of the table. Children were expected to eat silently, quickly, and without asking for anything. The salt shaker was often a boundary between the parents on one side of the table and children and servants on the other side. Children and servants were said to be "below the salt," indicating a less-favored place.

Children and Education *(cont.)*

Home Learning

Most children were educated at home. They received on-the-job training as farmers and craftsmen. Boys often learned a trade by helping their fathers. Mothers taught their daughters to cook, sew, spin, and care for the home, although daughters often learned how to care for livestock, plant crops, and help in their father's occupation as well.

Some parents knew how to read and write and taught these skills to their children. Books were expensive and rare in most homes although most families did own a Bible. In the 1700s almanacs, newspapers, and some cheaper books became more common.

Apprenticeships

Sometimes very young children became apprentices, and it was quite common for a boy of 10 or 11 to be apprenticed to a craftsman in order to learn a trade. The apprentice lived with the master and was fed by him. The master had complete power over an apprentice, who could be punished or whipped for disobedience or doing a job poorly. Children were apprenticed to become candle makers, tanners, wagon builders, silversmiths, printers, glass blowers, and many other trades. Ben Franklin, for example, learned his trade as a printer when he was apprenticed to his older brother.

New England Schools

Massachusetts passed a law in 1642 that required parents to teach their children to read. In 1647 Massachusetts required that every town with 50 families set up a school that all children could attend. Some private grade schools and academies were started even before that. Education was considered important so that people could read the Bible and participate in church activities.

Because paper was rare and expensive, there were few books. Children learned from primers and a *hornbook*. A piece of paper with the alphabet, the Lord's Prayer, Roman numerals, or the like was covered by a transparent sheet of cow horn and mounted on a piece of wood with a handle at one end for the child to hold.

Children and Education *(cont.)*

Higher Education

Quite a few of the original leaders of New England were college-educated men. Harvard College in Massachusetts was established in 1636. It was supported by a tax on the general populace. Latin grammar schools, both public and private, prepared students for college and offered classes in religion, mathematics, Latin, Greek, and English composition. Some academies were established in the 1700s to provide specialized education in practical subjects. Some academies allowed girls or were established for girls only. However, none of the half-dozen colleges in the colonial period admitted women.

Education in the Middle Colonies

The middle colonies offered some opportunities for children to be educated, but publicly financed schools were not required as in Massachusetts. Parents desiring to improve their station in life and who wanted their children to be successful sent their children to local, private schools. One of the most common books in these schools was the *New England Primer.* It was first published in the 1690s and had the Ten Commandments, some religious instruction, rhymes for the alphabet, and similar material. Good penmanship was considered a mark of an educated man. A few colleges had started in these colonies.

Education in the Southern Colonies

Southern educational experiences were much more rare. The sons of wealthy planters went to college in Europe or to William and Mary College, founded in 1693. There were few opportunities for poor or middle class children to receive even a grade-school education, although this improved somewhat in the 1700s.

It was illegal in most southern states to teach slaves to read and write. Owners feared that education would make the slaves realize how badly they were treated and encourage them to escape or revolt. However, some slave owners did teach their slaves.

Native Americans and New Settlers

Land Use

In every colony the basic conflict between the colonists and the Native Americans involved land. Indians of every tribe had been accustomed to living on and using the land freely. Many tribes planted some crops, but they also hunted and fished over wide areas. The white colonists fenced off their land, dug up the earth, and destroyed the hunting grounds.

Even when the whites purchased land from the Indians—usually for things of little real value—the Indians were only conceding the right of the colonists to use the land as they did themselves. The Indians did not have a sense of land ownership that allowed people to exclude others from using it, too.

Penn's Attitude

Some colonies had more enlightened Indian policies. William Penn actually did buy land from the Indians, and he insisted that they be treated fairly. The Quaker people who settled Pennsylvania usually had respect for their Indian neighbors. Roger Williams not only purchased Rhode Island land from the Narraganset Indians but also lived with them one winter and learned their language. He was respectful of their culture, and they appreciated his attitude.

Indian Guides

Some colonies would never have succeeded without the help of Native Americans. The Pilgrims who came on the Mayflower would probably not have survived if they had not been fortunate enough to meet Squanto, an Indian who had been kidnapped and taken to England years earlier. He spoke English and showed the new settlers which crops to plant and how to plant them in the cold New England climate. He also helped them fish and find clams. These Pilgrims also were able to make friends with Massasoit, chief of the Wampanoag tribe. The settlers of Jamestown learned to survive from their Indian neighbors as well. The Indians introduced them to new foods and traded with them when they needed food.

Native Americans and New Settlers *(cont.)*

Trade

When European settlers and Indians met, they usually exchanged gifts and engaged in trade. The colonists wanted food, furs, and sometimes information. The Native Americans were especially attracted to guns, hatchets, steel knives, cloth, beads, and glass objects. Indians often became dependent on these European products and stopped using their native weapons, clothes, and tools.

Some tribes became very dependent on firearms and ammunition. Guns gave a tribe enormous military advantages over tribes that had less access to firearms. When the Mohawk Indians acquired weapons from their Dutch neighbors in New York, for example, they achieved great power over the Algonquian tribes in their homeland.

Sometimes trade also helped to cement alliances between Europeans and Indian tribes. Hatred for the French coupled with English trade kept the powerful Iroquois confederacy strongly supportive of the English during the French and Indian War and also during the American Revolution.

Disease

The clash of cultures between the Europeans and the Native Americans had a severe impact on most tribes. Diseases such as smallpox, measles, and influenza wiped out entire villages because the native people had no immunity to diseases they had never encountered. During the 150 years of colonization, more Indians died of disease than from any other cause. These epidemics spread through large areas and sometimes decimated whole tribes.

Conflict

Many Indians and whites reached the same conclusion. They understood that the whites were unwilling and unable to truly live in peace and share the land. Sometimes a colony deliberately determined to drive the Indians off the land. Some whites used racism or religion as an excuse to kill the Indians. As a result, some Indians became violently opposed to the culture and existence of the Europeans.

Native Americans and New Settlers *(cont.)*

Wars

There were frequent skirmishes between individual colonists and Indians, and local communities often came to blows with neighboring tribes. Some conflicts were more generalized. Puritans attempting to settle the Connecticut Valley in the 1630s were opposed by the Pequot tribe that lived there. After several raids by both sides, the settlers attacked and burned Pequot villages with the aid of a tribal enemy, killing more than 500 Pequots of all ages.

King Philip's War

In the 1670s the Wampanoag tribe led by Metacom, who was called King Philip by the settlers, revolted against the constant encroachment on their land by the settlers of Plymouth colony. Philip was the son of their longtime friend Massasoit, who had tried to live in peace with the Pilgrim settlers. The Indians attacked more than 50 towns, killed more than 800 settlers, and threatened the survival of the colony.

Colonial leaders enlisted the aide of Mohawk Indians and other Indians who had converted to Christianity. After several bitter battles, Metacom was killed, his followers defeated, and many of his tribesmen sold into slavery. As many as 3,000 Indians were killed. This ended King Philip's War but only increased hostility between whites and Native Americans in New England. The peaceful Narraganset Indians were attacked and massacred on their own land because the settlers now feared all Indians.

Powhatan and Pocahontas

The settlers at Jamestown had settled on the land of a powerful confederation led by Powhatan, who led approximately 30,000 Indians. Powhatan was never certain how to treat these settlers. He did learn to respect their leader, John Smith, but he quickly began to fear the encroachment of these whites on his land. The story of his daughter Pocahontas illustrates some of the highs and lows of the Indian-settler relationship. Pocahantas saved Smith's life, was kidnapped by settlers, later converted to Christianity, married a settler named John Rolfe, and later died of smallpox.

Native Americans and New Settlers *(cont.)*

Jamestown Massacre

Opechancanough was Pocahontas's uncle and a *sachem*, or wise man, of his people. In 1622 he decided to destroy Jamestown and annihilate the whites. He led a massacre of as many as 1,200 settlers in the area. Only the warning of a friendly Christian convert from the tribe saved Jamestown from complete destruction. The massacre led to revenge killings by the settlers, attacks on some Indian villages, and hatred on both sides. In 1644 Opechancanough tried unsuccessfully to destroy Jamestown again. He was old and feeble, but his hatred still burned.

Depopulation

In 1607 when the English landed in Jamestown, the Native American population of North America east of the Mississippi River was about one million people. By the 1670s most of the Indians living in the English colonies had died from disease or warfare or had been pushed off of their lands. Many of the remaining Indians had moved west into areas where other Indian tribes already lived, or they had been settled into areas reserved for Indians.

By 1750 the Indian population had declined to about 150,000. In the New England colonies alone, the number of Indians declined from about 100,000 to 10,000. By comparison the colonies had grown to about 143,000 whites and 7,000 blacks by 1680. In the next 100 years, white European settlers numbered over two million, and there were more than half a million blacks.

Indentured Servitude and Slavery

Indentured Servants

One way for a poor young man in the British Isles to get to the New World was to become an indentured servant. These "bound men" were usually young men between the ages of 15 and 25 who signed a contract to work for five to seven years in exchange for passage to the colonies. By some estimates, as many as half of all the British immigrants to the colonies after the 1630s came as indentured servants.

During their time of indenture, these servants lived with the family that bought their contract. They often worked as field hands or occasionally as house servants, especially in the Chesapeake colonies of Maryland and Virginia. Sometimes they were treated humanely and sometimes as slaves. Maryland required that indentured servants who completed their contracts be given 50 acres of land, some tools, and seeds.

Women and children and even entire families were indentured. If a husband died at sea on the voyage over, his widow was assessed the terms of his indenture as well as her own. Poor orphans in London were often sent as indentured servants. Children were bound to work for their master until they turned 21. They often served as apprentices to their master, learning a trade in exchange for their unpaid labor. Some owners taught children to read as well as a trade and occasionally befriended them when they came of age and were ready to start work on their own.

Throughout the 1700s, many immigrants came to America from Europe through the indentured system.

Almost Slavery

Being bound to a cruel or stingy owner could be extremely depressing as it was very close to a slave's existence. Children and young adults often ran away from their owners and could be caught by the authorities and sent back. Often, an indentured servant was so poor and job prospects were so few at the end of his term of service that the only thing some could do was accept another indenture.

Indentured Servitude and Slavery *(cont.)*

Indian Slaves

English settlers tried to enslave captured Indians without much success. Tens of thousands of Indians were enslaved after major conflicts, such as the Pequot War in Connecticut and the battles with the Tuscarora Indians in North Carolina. Indian slavery was usually unsuccessful because Indian laborers often refused to work and died from starvation, beatings, and depression. It was also easier for Native Americans to escape from their white owners because they were able to survive in the wilderness and were often near villages that would shelter them when they escaped.

African Holocaust

At the time Columbus discovered the New World, the population of Africa was about the same as the population of Europe, a little over 50 million people. In the period between 1526 and 1870, at least 10 million Africans were captured, enslaved, and taken to Europe and the Americas. Approximately 400,000 African slaves were brought to English colonies and America. Millions more were sent to the Middle East and Asia. It was a true holocaust affecting communities throughout Africa.

Seedbed for Slavery

Tobacco was the catalyst for the rise of African slavery in the English colonies. It took nearly all year to raise and harvest the plants and required a great deal of manual labor. Tobacco was a very profitable cash crop for the settlers at Jamestown and the later colonies. The settlers quickly realized that they needed a source of cheap labor. Cultivation of other cash crops such as rice, indigo, sugar cane, and cotton also required cheap labor, and the plantation system of slavery was quickly adopted.

Indentured Servitude and Slavery *(cont.)*

Growth of African Slavery

The first 20 Africans arrived in America on a Dutch warship in 1619. At first they were treated as indentured servants, but the law and social practice soon came to regard these men and future African arrivals as permanent slaves. In 1640 (just 20 years later) there were about 150 black slaves in Virginia, and by 1650 the number had increased to 300. By 1700 there were about 28,000 African slaves in the colonies.

From 1660 onward, slavery spread quickly through the colonies. A 1662 Virginia law declared that all Africans would remain slaves for life. Male slaves outnumbered females about three to one in the 1600s. Using modern money terms, a slave in the late 1600s cost about $25 to buy in Africa and could be sold in the Americas for $150. Since white laborers cost about 70 cents a day, a slave paid for himself over a period of seven to eight months.

Trade Triangle

Slaves were considered trade goods, and they were an integral part of the triangular trade pattern in the colonies. The colonies exported cash crops such as rice, indigo, and tobacco to England. Sugar and molasses were exported to the West Indies, and slaves were imported from Africa.

The total black population was about 550,000 in the 1770s, which was about 20% of the total population. Several thousand slaves lived in the northern colonies and worked on farms or as domestic servants and artisans.

Close to 90% of the slaves lived in the southern colonies, usually on plantations. Up to 8% of the blacks in the 1770s were living as free men, usually in the northern colonies.

The Middle Passage

The *Middle Passage* is the term used for the journey of African slaves across the Atlantic Ocean to the New World. Slaves who had already been captured in tribal warfare or kidnapped from their villages by African or Arab slave catchers were often marched hundreds of miles to the coast and sold to sea-going slave traders from Europe or America.

Indentured Servitude and Slavery *(cont.)*

Aboard Ship

Male slaves often wore spiked iron collars, and slaves were branded like cattle to prove ownership. Once on board ship, Africans were afraid that the white crew would eat them or drink their blood. The death rate was usually about 20% on most voyages but could reach as high as 50% on some ships. Men were shackled hand and feet to prevent escape, revolt, or suicide by drowning.

All of the African slaves were held in tightly packed quarters in savage conditions. The ship's slave quarters had a foul stench, little air, very little drinkable water, and meager amounts of food. To keep the slaves healthy and exercised, they were brought on deck to dance to the music of one of the crew. People who did not exercise enough were whipped.

Slave Life in the Colonies

Slave prisons and slave markets were the holding pens and distribution centers for slaves in the colonies. Men were separated from their wives and children and often sold separately without regard for family bonds. Slaves were examined and marketed like cattle.

Gang labor was a common labor practice. A group of slaves worked the fields under the watchful eye of a harsh overseer. Field hands were less valuable in the social and economic context of Southern slavery than were domestic servants or urban slaves, who sometimes had acquired skills as craftsmen. Few male slaves had duties in an owner's house.

Slaves usually owned no property, were forbidden to learn how to read and write, could not be witnesses in a court, and had no personal rights—regardless of how cruelly they were treated by an owner or any other white. Owners whipped, brutalized, and killed slaves as they wished. Slaves were fed, clothed, and housed in the cheapest manner possible. Plantation owners encouraged women to have many children because children provided an endless source of cheap new slaves. Slave children usually started work by the age of seven.

Slave rebellions terrified plantation owners. A rebellion in 1712 occurred in New York. Other rebellions and conspiracies to revolt occurred throughout the colonies, including in South Carolina in 1729 and in 1730 in Virginia, but these were put down with great force and brutality.

Colonial Leaders

John Smith

John Smith was a true adventurer. He ran away to sea as a boy, fought against the Turks, became a Hungarian hero for his bravery against the Turks, and was captured and enslaved. He killed his master and escaped to wander through Russia, Poland, and Germany and then ended up fighting pirates in North Africa.

In 1607 Captain Smith sailed to Virginia and established Jamestown, the first permanent English colony in North America. Only 28 years old, he was responsible for saving the settlement from destruction and failure. His motto as leader was simple: "If you don't work, you don't eat." He forced the gentlemen who had come to Jamestown looking for gold and easy riches to work if they wanted to survive. Smith was also able to maintain an uneasy peace with the Indians under the powerful leader Powhatan.

While exploring the Chesapeake area, he was stung by a deadly stingray and was expected to die. His grave was even dug. He survived this and many other dangers, including being injured in a gunpowder explosion and then nearly drowning. In 1609 he returned to England. Before Smith left, the colony had provisions and seemed on the road to success. Years later, John Smith returned to America and mapped the New England coast.

Pocahontas

Pocahontas was the favorite daughter of Powhatan, the powerful leader of the Indian tribes in the coastal areas from the Chesapeake Bay through eastern Virginia to the North Carolina border. Pocahontas was fascinated by John Smith and twice saved his life. In one instance, she laid her head across his chest to protect him.

After being kidnapped by the settlers, Pocahontas fell in love with and married John Rolfe, a plantation owner. Although her father did not attend the wedding, the marriage did help to cement a peace between the settlers and Powhatan Indians. After she had a baby, Rolfe decided to take his family to England where Pocahontas became known as Lady Rebecca and was treated like a princess. As they prepared to return to Virginia, Pocahontas contracted smallpox and died at the age of 22.

Colonial Leaders *(cont.)*

John Winthrop

John Winthrop was a Puritan who lost his job as a lawyer in England because his religious views were opposed to the established Church of England. After coming to the New World, he helped found the city of Boston and became the first governor of the Massachusetts Bay Colony. Winthrop hoped to make his colony a "city on a hill," a god-fearing community that would be a model to other communities. Religious dissenters in his colony, especially Roger Williams and Anne Hutchinson, troubled Winthrop.

Roger Williams

Roger Williams was a Puritan minister with an independent streak. He did not think other settlers in Massachusetts should have to practice religion as the Puritans did. He also did not believe that Indians should be indiscriminately killed or forced to convert to Christianity. Williams became such a thorn in the side of the Puritan leaders of the Massachusetts colony that he was banished from the colony and ordered back to England.

Williams, however, chose to escape and went south to Rhode Island where he founded the city of Providence and the colony of Rhode Island. He made friends with the neighboring Narraganset Indians, learned their language, and paid the tribe for lands settled by whites. Williams strongly believed in the rights of the Indians and practiced what he preached. He believed in freedom of conscience and allowed people of many faiths, including Quakers and Jews, to settle in his colony. He also respected the religions of the Indian peoples.

Anne Hutchinson

Anne Hutchinson was a religious dissenter who annoyed the Puritan leaders of Massachusetts to no end with her independent opinions, sharp tongue, and stubborn insistence on speaking her mind. She claimed God was guiding her. Although some people supported Hutchinson, others thought she should be quiet and take care of her 14 children. The Puritan leaders finally lost patience with her and threw her out of the Puritan church and the Massachusetts colony. Hutchinson moved to Rhode Island and later to New York, where she was killed by Indians.

Colonial Leaders *(cont.)*

Mary Dyer

Mary Dyer was a pious Puritan who began to speak her own mind like her friend, Anne Hutchinson. She became a Quaker and eventually irritated the leadership of Massachusetts so much that she was tried and sentenced to be hanged. At the last minute, her life was spared and she was banished instead. Dyer went to Rhode Island for a time and then returned to Massachusetts and started preaching again. She was tried again and offered banishment from the colony again, but she refused and was hanged.

Olaudah Equiano

Olaudah Equiano wrote one of the very few accounts of life as a slave, detailing his experiences from the time he was kidnapped in Nigeria at age 11 until he achieved his freedom. Equiano was brought across the Atlantic Ocean on a slave ship bound for the West Indies. A series of fortunate events landed him as a slave to a Quaker merchant, who later let him buy his freedom. Equiano eventually moved to England, where he adopted the dress and manners of an English gentleman. His explicit account of his ordeal as a slave convinced many readers of the evils of the slave trade.

William Bradford

William Bradford was the second governor of the Plymouth Colony. His leadership was so essential to the colony's survival that he was re-elected 30 times. He invited Chief Massasoit and his Wampanoag people to a Thanksgiving feast in gratitude for the settlers' harvest the first year. Bradford insisted that the colonists treat the Indians fairly. The peace treaty he made with Chief Massasoit lasted over 50 years despite some incidents of bad faith. Bradford also recorded the early history of the colony.

William Penn

William Penn was a Quaker who founded the colony of Pennsylvania as a holy experiment where Quakers and other religious dissidents could live and practice their religious beliefs. He received the land as repayment for a debt King Charles II owed his father. Penn negotiated with the Indians and paid for the use of the land. He established the Charter of Liberties and Privileges of 1701, which allowed the people to govern themselves and prevented anyone—including himself—from becoming too powerful.

Colonial Leaders *(cont.)*

Eliza Lucas Pinckney

Eliza Lucas Pinckney took charge of her father's South Carolina plantations when she was 16 while he went off to join his English regiment in a war against Spain. Eliza managed the business of three plantations and became convinced that indigo, a blue dye used on cloth, would make a good cash crop to grow along with rice. She experimented for years with various methods of planting and production and succeeded not only in producing a crop for herself but encouraging her neighbors to do likewise. Eliza also experimented with other crops such as figs and silkworms. At the age of 22, she fell in love with and married a 45-year-old widower named Charles Pinckney. Eliza and her children would become important leaders in the movement for colonial independence.

Benjamin Franklin

Benjamin Franklin is one of the most important leaders in American history. Born in 1706 in Boston, Massachusetts, Franklin was the fifteenth of 17 children of a candle and soap maker. He had some occasional schooling and was apprenticed by his father to his half brother James to learn the printing trade. After quarreling with James, Ben ran away and eventually settled in Philadelphia, where he gradually achieved success as a printer through good fortune and hard work. His newspaper and publication *Poor Richard's Almanac* made him a very wealthy man.

Franklin's many accomplishments included helping to create the first fire department in Philadelphia, a library, the academy that eventually became the University of Pennsylvania, and an efficient post office system. He became an agent for Pennsylvania and other colonies in England before the war. Franklin was an early believer in colonial unity and independence from England. He became an amateur scientist with a worldwide reputation. In addition to his famous kite experiment that proved lightning was a form of electricity, Franklin invented the lightning rod and bifocal glasses.

Powhatan (Wahunsonacock)

Powhatan was the chief of the powerful Powhatan tribe that lived near Jamestown, Virginia. He alternated between offering help and trying to destroy the settlement. He did learn to trust Captain John Smith and even negotiated with him. His favorite daughter was Pocahontas.

Colonial Leaders *(cont.)*

James Oglethorpe

A member of Parliament for over 30 years, James Oglethorpe was an idealist who believed that people could start a new life in the New World. He founded the colony of Georgia as a haven for debtors, prisoners, and the poor. He also saw that Georgia could be a buffer to protect the colony of South Carolina from incursions and attacks from Spanish-owned Florida. As leader of the colony, Oglethorpe led a number of raids against the Spanish and even tried to capture St. Augustine from the Spanish. When the people of Georgia became discontented with his leadership and ideals, which included opposition to slavery and alcohol, he was recalled to England.

Squanto

Squanto was an Indian from the Wampanoag tribe in Massachusetts who had been kidnapped from his tribe by white explorers and taken to England, where he learned English. After a series of adventures, he was able to return to his native land. Squanto was instrumental in helping the starving Pilgrims at Plymouth Colony survive by teaching them how to grow corn, beans, pumpkins, and squash in the short New England summer. He also taught the colonists how to fish and find clams.

Chief Massasoit

Chief Massasoit of the Wampanoag tribe attended the first Thanksgiving celebration with the Pilgrims of Plymouth Colony. He was a serious leader who tried to maintain peace between his people and the settlers who were invading his land. He made a treaty of peace with Governor Bradford that lasted more than 50 years—despite the constant encroachment of settlers on Wampanoag land.

Peter Stuyvesant

Peter Stuyvesant was the Dutch governor of New Netherland who ran the colony with a firm hand for 20 years. He had lost a leg fighting the Portuguese in the West Indies and wore a wooden leg decorated with silver nails, which led to the nickname Old Silvernails. Stuyvesant wiped out a Swedish colony with which he had a dispute and governed the Dutch colony until the English captured New Amsterdam and renamed it New York.

King Philip (Metacom)

Metacom, called Philip by the English settlers, was the son of Massasoit and a chief of the Wampanoag tribe in New England. After continual encroachments on native lands by colonists, he broke with his father's efforts to keep peace with their white Massachusetts neighbors. Metacom led a massacre of English settlers and launched what came to be known as King Philip's War. After he was killed in 1676, the uprising was put down.

Founding the Colonies 1607–1636 Quiz

Directions: Read pages 8–10 about the founding of the English colonies. Answer each question below by circling the correct answer. Then underline the sentence in the article where the answer is found.

1. In which year was the colony of New Hampshire founded?
   a. 1636
   b. 1623
   c. 1607
   d. 1614

2. Where was the first permanent English colony founded?
   a. Virginia
   b. Massachusetts
   c. Connecticut
   d. Rhode Island

3. Which colony was founded by the Calvert family?
   a. Pennsylvania
   b. Maryland
   c. Jamestown
   d. Plymouth

4. Which colony gave full religious freedom to all settlers?
   a. Massachusetts
   b. Virginia
   c. Rhode Island
   d. Maryland

5. Which colony had the first representative assembly?
   a. Massachusetts
   b. Virginia
   c. Rhode Island
   d. New Hampshire

6. Maryland was founded as a haven for Catholics. What is a *haven*?
   a. a church
   b. a place of safety
   c. a plantation
   d. a colony

7. Which colonial leader insisted that any settler who wanted to eat must work?
   a. Roger Williams
   b. Thomas Hooker
   c. John Smith
   d. Peter Stuyvesant

8. Whose ideas were contained in the Fundamental Orders of Connecticut?
   a. Thomas Hooker
   b. John Smith
   c. Roger Williams
   d. Adriaen Black

9. Which colony was founded by John Mason?
   a. Maine
   b. New Hampshire
   c. Connecticut
   d. New York

10. Who bought the island of Manhattan for the city of New Amsterdam?
    a. Peter Stuyvesant
    b. Henry Hudson
    c. Charles II
    d. Peter Minuet

Founding the Colonies 1636–1733 Quiz

Directions: Read pages 11–13 about the founding of the English colonies. Answer each question below by circling the correct answer. Then underline the sentence in the article where the answer is found.

1. In which year did the two Carolinas become separate colonies?
   a. 1653
   b. 1663
   c. 1670
   d. 1712

2. Which colony was founded as a haven for Quakers?
   a. Delaware
   b. Pennsylvania
   c. New Jersey
   d. Georgia

3. For which group of people was the colony of Georgia founded?
   a. Quakers
   b. Catholics
   c. debtors
   d. orphans

4. To whom did King Charles give Carolana?
   a. William Penn
   b. James Oglethorpe
   c. lords proprietors
   d. Sir George Carteret

5. Which European settlers first founded a settlement in New Jersey?
   a. Swedes
   b. Dutch
   c. English
   d. Spanish

6. James Oglethorpe hoped to make Georgia a utopia. What is a utopia?
   a. a perfect place to live
   b. a home for strangers
   c. a religious center
   d. a prison

7. Which city means "The City of Brotherly Love"?
   a. Pennsylvania
   b. Philadelphia
   c. Savannah
   d. Charleston

8. Why did King Charles give Pennsylvania to William Penn?
   a. He owed Penn money.
   b. Charles was a Quaker
   c. to get rid of the land
   d. so that Penn would find gold

9. In which colony was the settlement at Roanoke Island attempted?
   a. North Carolina
   b. South Carolina
   c. Pennsylvania
   d. Georgia

10. In which colony were the first log houses built by settlers?
    a. New Jersey
    b. North Carolina
    c. Delaware
    d. Pennsylvania

Colonial Lifestyles Quiz

Directions: Read pages 14–16 about colonial lifestyles. Answer each question below by circling the correct answer. Then underline the sentence in the article where the answer is found.

1. What was the name of the powerful Indian confederation in the middle colonies?
   a. Algonquian
   b. Iroquois
   c. Powhatan
   d. Delaware

2. What is the name of the punishment device that consisted of an iron mask with an iron tongue?
   a. pillory
   b. ducking stool
   c. stocks
   d. gossip's bridle

3. Which of these was not a New England colony?
   a. New York
   b. Massachusetts
   c. New Hampshire
   d. Connecticut

4. What is *indigo*?
   a. a kind of wheat
   b. a punishment for gossiping
   c. a blue dye
   d. a tree

5. How often did colonists usually bathe?
   a. daily
   b. once a week
   c. very rarely
   d. once a month

6. What was the fastest method of travel in colonial days?
   a. by water
   b. stagecoach
   c. walking
   d. on horseback

7. Which of the following was not a southern colony?
   a. North Carolina
   b. Maryland
   c. Georgia
   d. Florida

8. In which colony is Charleston located?
   a. North Carolina
   b. Georgia
   c. South Carolina
   d. Virginia

9. Where did settlers from Sweden, Scotland, Germany, and the Netherlands most often settle?
   a. the southern colonies
   b. New England
   c. the middle colonies
   d. Massachusetts

10. Which form of punishment was most favored for scolds, nagging women, and quarrelsome couples?
    a. pillory
    b. ducking stool
    c. branding
    d. whipping post

Children and Education Quiz

Directions: Read pages 17–19 about children and education in colonial times. Answer each question below by circling the correct answer. Then underline the sentence in the article where the answer is found.

1. Which state passed a law in 1642 requiring parents to teach their children to read?
   a. Massachusetts
   b. Maryland
   c. Rhode Island
   d. Connecticut

2. When did children usually get up in the morning?
   a. 8 o'clock
   b. dawn
   c. 6 o'clock
   d. noon

3. What is the name of paper with the alphabet on one side and a prayer on the other under a piece of cow horn?
   a. primer
   b. Bible
   c. dictionary
   d. hornbook

4. What was the most common book in most schools?
   a. *Bible*
   b. *Ten Commandments*
   c. *New England Primer*
   d. *Poor Richard's Almanac*

5. Who sat "below the salt"?
   a. parents
   b. adults
   c. children
   d. teachers

6. Who was most likely to become apprentices?
   a. 10-year-old girls
   b. African children
   c. 18-year-old boys
   d. 10-year-old boys

7. In what year did Massachusetts require public schools in all communities of 50 families or more?
   a. 1642
   b. 1647
   c. 1636
   d. 1693

8. In what year was Harvard College founded?
   a. 1636
   b. 1647
   c. 1693
   d. 1642

9. Which children's game involved tossing a ring over a stake?
   a. walking on stilts
   b. quoits
   c. bowling
   d. charades

10. Which of the following would children *not* do while eating?
    a. eat quickly
    b. eat silently
    c. talk
    d. stand behind a parent

Native Americans and New Settlers Quiz

Directions: Read pages 20–23 about the conflicts between Native Americans and the new settlers. Answer each question below by circling the correct answer. Then underline the sentence in the article where the answer is found.

1. Which sachem tried to destroy Jamestown?
   a. Pocahontas
   b. Opechancanough
   c. King Philip
   d. Powhatan

2. Which chief was Pocahontas' father?
   a. Massasoit
   b. Opechancanough
   c. Powhatan
   d. Metacom

3. Which was the major cause of conflict between the settlers and Native Americans?
   a. trade
   b. disease
   c. land
   d. religion

4. How many Indians were killed in King Philip's War?
   a. 3,000
   b. 30,000
   c. 500
   d. 1,200

5. Which colonial leader bought land from the Indians and wanted them treated fairly?
   a. William Penn
   b. John Rolfe
   c. John Smith
   d. King Philip

6. Which was the most sought after trade item by the Indians?
   a. knives
   b. cloth
   c. firearms
   d. beads

7. Which Native American confederation strongly supported the English against the French?
   a. Algonquian
   b. Powhatan
   c. Narraganset
   d. Iroquois

8. What was King Philip's Indian name?
   a. Metacom
   b. Massasoit
   c. Opechancanough
   d. Pequot

9. Which was the primary cause of Native American deaths?
   a. war
   b. slavery
   c. disease
   d. starvation

10. What was the Native American population east of the Mississippi River in 1607?
    a. 150,000
    b. 1,000,000
    c. 100,000
    d. 10,000

Indentured Servitude and Slavery Quiz

Directions: Read pages 24–27 about indentured servitude and slavery in the colonies. Answer each question below by circling the correct answer. Then underline the sentence in the article where the answer is found.

1. At what age were indentured children freed?
   a. 21
   b. 18
   c. 25
   d. 16

2. What was the usual term of service for an indentured servant?
   a. 10 years
   b. 5 to 7 months
   c. 5 to 7 years
   d. life

3. What was the catalyst for the rise of Negro slavery in the English colonies?
   a. agriculture
   b. tobacco
   c. rice farming
   d. indentured servitude

4. How many slaves were brought to the English colonies and the United States between 1526 and 1870?
   a. 400,000
   b. 4 million
   c. 10 million
   d. 50 million

5. In modern money terms what was the price of a slave in the Americas in the late 1600s?
   a. $25
   b. $500
   c. 70 cents
   d. $150

6. What name is given to the voyage of slaves across the Atlantic Ocean?
   a. indenture
   b. Middle Passage
   c. triangular trade
   d. holocaust

7. At what age did slave children start working on a plantation?
   a. 21
   b. 12
   c. 7
   d. 18

8. About how many people lived in Africa in Columbus's time?
   a. 10 million
   b. 4 million
   c. 50 million
   d. 400,000

9. What is the trade pattern that involved the sale of goods to Europe and the West Indies and slaves to the colonies?
   a. Middle Passage
   b. indentured servitude
   c. triangular trade
   d. agriculture

10. Which kind of slavery was unsuccessful because the slaves refused to work?
    a. Indian
    b. African
    c. indentured servitude
    d. apprenticeship

Colonial Leaders Quiz

Directions: Read pages 28–32 about colonial leaders. Answer each question below by circling the correct answer. Then underline the sentence in the article where the answer is found.

1. Who founded a colony for Quakers to settle?
   a. William Bradford
   b. William Penn
   c. John Smith
   d. John Winthrop

2. Who told the men in his colony, "If you don't work, you don't eat"?
   a. John Smith
   b. Roger Williams
   c. John Winthrop
   d. James Oglethorpe

3. Who founded the colony of Georgia as a settlement for debtors?
   a. Roger Williams
   b. James Oglethorpe
   c. William Bradford
   d. Peter Stuyvesant

4. Who was called Old Silvernails?
   a. Massasoit
   b. Peter Stuyvesant
   c. John Winthrop
   d. William Bradford

5. Which Wampanoag chief made a longstanding peace treaty with the Pilgrims at Plymouth Colony?
   a. Pocahontas
   b. Metacom
   c. Massasoit
   d. Squanto

6. Which leader founded the colony of Rhode Island?
   a. William Bradford
   b. Peter Stuyvesant
   c. Anne Hutchinson
   d. Roger Williams

7. Which Puritan leader was hanged for expressing unpopular religious opinions?
   a. Anne Hutchinson
   b. Olaudah Equiano
   c. Mary Dyer
   d. Roger Williams

8. Who successfully experimented with raising indigo?
   a. Eliza Pinckney
   b. Mary Dyer
   c. Pocahontas
   d. Anne Hutchinson

9. Who invented the lightning rod and bifocal glasses?
   a. Benjamin Franklin
   b. William Bradford
   c. John Smith
   d. William Penn

10. Who was Lady Rebecca?
    a. Anne Hutchinson
    b. Mary Dyer
    c. Pocahontas
    d. Eliza Pinckney

Teacher Lesson Plans for Language Arts

Vocabulary, Facts and Opinions, Native Words

Objectives: Students will apply language arts skills in vocabulary enrichment and discern between opinions and facts.

Materials: copies of Colonial Terms (page 43); articles in newspapers or magazines; copies of Fact Versus Opinion (page 44); copies of Native American Words (page 45); map of the United States or list of U.S. states

Procedure

1. Reproduce and distribute Colonial Terms (page 43). Review the vocabulary and pronunciation if necessary. Have students complete the assigned page.

2. Reproduce and distribute Fact Versus Opinion (page 44). Review the concepts of fact and opinion. Have students read an article and do the article analysis.

3. Reproduce and distribute Native American Words (page 45). Review the words and pronunciation if necessary. Have students use a map of the United States or a list of the state names and guess which states have Indian names.

Assessment: Correct the activity sheets together. Have students check the names of local places for Indian or foreign origins.

Letter Writing and "How To" Essay

Objective: Students will develop skills in writing letters and essays.

Materials: copies of Writing History: Letter Writing (page 46); copies of Writing a "How To" Essay (page 47); copies of "How To" Essay Outline (page 48)

Procedure

1. Reproduce and distribute Writing History: Letter Writing (page 46). Review the instructions and suggested topics. Review the letter and envelope formats. Have students complete the assignment.

2. Reproduce and distribute Writing a "How To" Essay (page 47) and "How To" Essay Outline (page 48). Review the purpose of a "how to" essay, and discuss suggested topics with students. Explain the structure of the essay and give examples. Students can use the work sheet to prewrite their essay.

Assessment: Have students publish and post their letters and share their essays with the class.

Teacher Lesson Plans for Language Arts *(cont.)*

Journals and Literature

Objectives: Students will read from and respond to a variety of fictional and biographical accounts of the colonial era. They will be able to recognize the elements of a story with historical fiction. Students will learn to keep journals.

Materials: copies of *The Journal of Jasper Jonathan Pierce* (page 49); copies of Writing History: Keeping a Journal (page 46); copies of Focus on Author Ann Rinaldi (page 50); copies of Elements of a Story (page 53); literature selections mentioned on the pages in this section including *The Journal of Jasper Jonathan Pierce* and the other Ann Rinaldi books listed on page 50

Procedure

1. Reproduce and distribute *The Journal of Jasper Jonathan Pierce* activity (page 49). Review the assignment, and have students answer the comprehension questions. Help students get started on the discussion questions in the Extension activity.
2. Reproduce and distribute Writing History: Keeping a Journal (page 46). Review the concept of the journal, brainstorm journal topics, and have students begin their journals on the activity page.
3. Reproduce and distribute Focus on Author Ann Rinaldi (page 50). Assign the books to individuals, a reading circle group, or the class, depending on your supply of books and the reading abilities of your students.
4. Reproduce and distribute Elements of a Story (page 53). Teach or review the elements of a story. Use *The Journal of Jasper Jonathan Pierce* or any other familiar book as an example. Have students apply the Elements of a Story to the Ann Rinaldi book they read.

Assessment: Have students share their comprehension activities and story evaluations with their reading group or the entire class.

Historical Fiction

Objective: Students will read from and respond to fictional and biographical accounts of the colonial era.

Materials: copies of *The Serpent Never Sleeps* (pages 51 and 52); copies of *The Double Life of Pocahontas* (pages 54 and 55); literature selections mentioned on the pages in this section including *The Serpent Never Sleeps* by Scott O'Dell and *The Double Life of Pocahontas* by Jean Fritz; other literary selections by Scott O'Dell (page 52) and by Jean Fritz (page 55)

Procedure

1. Reproduce and distribute *The Serpent Never Sleeps* activity (pages 51 and 52). Have students read the book independently, in small groups, or as a class. Review the assignment, and have students answer the questions. Allow them to discuss the extension questions. Encourage students to read other books by Scott O'Dell.
2. Reproduce and distribute *The Double Life of Pocahontas* activity sheets (pages 54 and 55). This book is a very good read-aloud piece, or students may read it independently. Review the assignment, and instruct students to answer the questions after reading the book. Have them discuss the extension questions. Encourage students to read other books by Jean Fritz.

Assessment: Have students share their comprehension activities and discussion activities with their reading group or the entire class.

Teacher Lesson Plans for Language Arts *(cont.)*

Readers' Theater

Objective: Students will learn to use their voices effectively in dramatic reading.

Materials: copies of Readers' Theater Notes (page 56) and copies of The Starving Time (pages 57 and 58)

Procedure

1. Review the basic concept of Readers' Theater with the class. Use the Readers' Theater Notes (page 56) to emphasize the important skills.

2. Have students read over The Starving Time (pages 57 and 58). Place students in small groups and allow time to practice reading the script over several days.

3. Schedule class performances, and have students share the prepared script.

4. Then, use the suggestions on the bottom of Readers' Theater Notes (page 56) to assign topics to teams of students. Allow student teams time to create and practice their scripts.

5. Schedule classroom performances of these scripts.

Assessment: Base performance assessments on pacing, volume, expression, and focus of the participants. Student-created scripts should demonstrate general writing skills, dramatic tension, and a good plot.

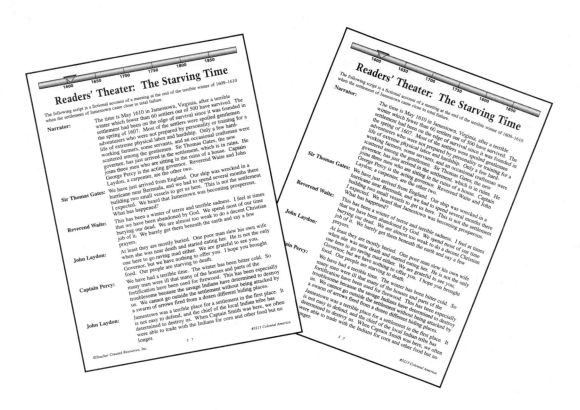

Colonial Terms

Directions: Match each word in Column 1 with its correct meaning in Column 2. Use a dictionary, the glossary at the end of the book, and student-reading pages to help you define these words related to the birth of the United States.

Column 1

_____ 1. **apprentice**

_____ 2. **colony**

_____ 3. **debtor**

_____ 4. **found**

_____ 5. **hornbook**

_____ 6. **indigo**

_____ 7. **massacre**

_____ 8. **plunder**

_____ 9. **population**

_____ 10. **primer**

Column 2

a. to steal and destroy

b. to start a colony

c. killing many people

d. a plant which produces blue dye

e. territory owned by another nation

f. book used to teach reading

g. board used to teach the alphabet

h. a person who owes money

i. number of people in an area

j. a person learning a craft

Directions: Write the word from the following list that matches each definition.

Word List

Burgesses	Parliament	Puritans
indentured servants	Pilgrims	Quakers
Iroquois	Powhatans	Wampanoags
lords proprietors		

_____ 11. religious dissenters who wanted to reform the Church of England

_____ 12. members of the five nations Indian confederation in New York

_____ 13. people who agree to work for several years to pay for their passage

_____ 14. members of the Society of Friends

_____ 15. settlers at Plymouth Colony

_____ 16. powerful New England Indian tribe

_____ 17. rich men given land grants

_____ 18. elected representatives in Virginia

_____ 19. England's lawmakers

_____ 20. powerful alliance of tribes in Virginia

Fact Versus Opinion

Newspapers in colonial days were extremely opinionated. They expressed the opinions of the publisher and often questioned the motives of public leaders with whom they disagreed. Publications today are usually more balanced but often still express opinions as well as facts.

Facts are statements that can be objectively proven.

Example: George Washington was the first President of the United States.

Opinions are statements that express the ideas of the writer and are not necessarily true.

Example: George Washington was the best president of the United States.

Assignment

1. Read an article in a newspaper or magazine or on an Internet website. The article may be about any topic (sports, science, history, politics, environment, etc.).

2. Underline (or highlight with a marker) facts and opinions expressed in the article.

3. Complete the work sheet below, and then share what you wrote with a small group or the entire class.

Title of Article: _____

Author: _____

Publication: _____

Subject of the Article: _____

Brief Summary: _____

_____

_____

Three Facts Stated in the Article

1. _____

2. _____

3. _____

Three Opinions Stated in the Article

1. _____

2. _____

3. _____

Native American Words

Many Native American words have become a part of the American language. Some were the names of plants and animals, and others were names of places. Several of the words changed as they were heard and written by the settlers.

Assignment

Match each Native American word in Column 1 with its correct meaning in Column 2. Use dictionaries, books about Indians, and Internet sources to help you.

Column 1

_____ 1. **caucus**

_____ 2. **hickory**

_____ 3. **hominy**

_____ 4. **moccasin**

_____ 5. **okay**

_____ 6. **moose**

_____ 7. **pemmican**

_____ 8. **raccoon**

_____ 9. **squash**

_____ 10. **succotash**

_____ 11. **tamarack**

_____ 12. **totem**

Column 2

a. a masked mammal

b. a kind of larch tree

c. to agree

d. an animal or nature symbol

e. dried meat

f. a gourd

g. leather footwear

h. a tree with very hard wood

i. ground corn

j. a very large type of deer

k. cooked lima beans and corn

l. a political meeting

Challenge

In the United States, 26 states have Native American names. How many of these can you name?

1. _____

2. _____

3. _____

4. _____

5. _____

6. _____

7. _____

8. _____

9. _____

10. _____

11. _____

12. _____

13. _____

14. _____

15. _____

16. _____

17. _____

18. _____

19. _____

20. _____

21. _____

22. _____

23. _____

24. _____

25. _____

26. _____

Writing History

Letter Writing

In colonial days the only way to communicate with your friends or family over long distances was by letter. Telegraphs, telephones, computers, and the electronic marvels of the modern world were still far in the future. In fact, much of what we know about colonial lifestyles (and even about history) is from letters that have survived, written by both famous people and ordinary settlers.

Assignment

Pretend that you have no access to a telephone, computer, or any other modern means of communication. On another sheet of paper, write at least a five-paragraph letter to a friend or relative (real or imagined) who lives far away. The letter should discuss several of the topics listed below, giving as many details about each topic as you can.

Suggested Topics

- your best friend
- a funny thing that happened
- a typical school day
- a game or sport you play
- local events
- local clothes and fashions
- a book you read
- a place you visited
- favorite foods
- a hobby

Keeping a Journal

Many people keep journals to record their daily experiences, thoughts, ideas, and feelings. Sometimes journal writers record descriptions of people, places, or things. For example, someone interested in nature may include both written descriptions and artistic sketches of plants, animals, or landscapes. A journal may be in a diary format or kept in a spiral-bound notebook.

Assignment

Use a notebook to keep a journal for at least one week. It may be in a diary format about what is happening in your life or just some thoughts you have. Use the ideas below to help you think of what to write for your first few entries. Try to make an entry every day.

My Journal

Date: _____

Today I _____

At school I _____

I saw _____

I am feeling _____

I think that _____

Writing a "How To" Essay

American colonists were extremely interested in learning how to do things. They continually tried to acquire skills that would make their lives easier or more rewarding. They wanted to know how to create things better, more economically, or more efficiently. Whether it was Squanto teaching the Pilgrims how to grow crops in New England or Benjamin Franklin's improvements on the stove, the colonists were avid learners.

Assignment: Use the "How To" Essay Outline (page 48) to help you write a "how to" essay about one of the topics listed at the bottom of the page or one you are interested in or have experience doing. The essay should include an introduction, a body, and a conclusion.

1. **Introduction**—The introduction consists of an opening paragraph that clearly tells what you are going to describe and why it is important to know how to do this. Be enthusiastic, and grab the attention of your reader.

2. **Body**—The body of the essay should contain three or more paragraphs. Each paragraph should describe one step. Steps can be numbered, or transition words such as the following can be used:

   - first . . . second
   - next . . . then
   - before . . . afterwards
   - finally

3. **Conclusion**—The concluding paragraph should describe the final product and mention any special cautions, concerns, or likely problems.

Suggested Topics

- how to ride a skateboard
- how to bake a cake
- how to make a sandwich
- how to plant a garden
- how to care for a pet
- how to use a yo-yo
- how to play soccer

- how to fish
- how to tie shoes
- how to use a computer
- how to train a dog
- how to launder clothes
- how to play an instrument
- how to build a snowman

"How To" Essay Outline

Directions: Use the outline on this page to begin writing your "how to" essay.

_____
(Title)

Introduction

Topic: _____

Why you should learn how to: _____

_____

_____

Body

Step 1: _____

_____

_____

Step 2: _____

_____

_____

Step 3: _____

_____

_____

Step 4: _____

_____

_____

Step 5: _____

_____

_____

Conclusion

_____

_____

The Journal of Jasper Jonathan Pierce

Jasper Pierce is a "bound boy," an indentured servant who travels aboard the *Mayflower* to the New World with his master, a kind and understanding man. Jasper's keeps a journal, which is addressed to his brother Tom who remained in England. In the journal, Jasper tells about his adventures aboard ship and in the early days of the founding of Plymouth Colony.

Assignment

Read *The Journal of Jasper Jonathan Pierce* by Ann Rinaldi. Then answer the following questions on a separate sheet of paper.

1. How did Jasper become an orphan?
2. Why did Tom not come to Plymouth also?
3. What happened to Mrs. Bradford?
4. Who was the first Indian chief to visit the colony?
5. How did Squanto teach them to plant corn?
6. What happened to Squanto's tribe?
7. What did Jasper do with the first part of his journal?
8. Why did Dotey and Leister get into a duel?
9. Why did Tom run away from the colony?
10. Who fell in love with Priscilla?
11. Who are the Saints?
12. Who are the Strangers?
13. What is a *pinese*?
14. What skill did Jasper have that fascinated the Indians?
15. Who came to America as a "bound servant" to Mr. Hicks?

Extension

Discuss the following questions with a small group or the entire class.

1. Why did the Indians come to visit the settlement?
2. How did the Mayflower Compact help the colony get established?
3. Did the colony have good leadership? Who were the best leaders? Why?
4. Why did so many colonists die?
5. Did the Indians and settlers show good faith and trust in dealing with each other? Give examples.
6. Would you have been willing to be a "bound servant"? Why?
7. Is Constance really at fault for the duel between Dotey and Leister? Explain your reasons.

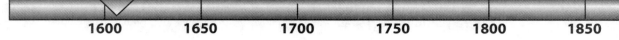

Focus on Author Ann Rinaldi

Ann Rinaldi is one of the most effective authors of historical fiction for young readers. Her novels are especially appealing to readers who like determined, headstrong, confident young heroines. Rinaldi's books are painstakingly accurate in detail and filled with the small details of life, which create a sharp edge of reality in her writing. Her novels are based on the lives of real individuals and peopled with interesting and important characters who actually lived during the period. Ann Rinaldi says her interest in writing historical fiction was sparked by her son Ron who loaned her many books from his library and "turned her on to history."

Hang a Thousand Trees With Ribbons (Harcourt, 1996) is the story of the life of Phillis Wheatley. This young slave was kidnapped from her native village by her father's enemies and made the dreadful crossing of the Atlantic Ocean, called the Middle Passage, where she saw her mother thrown overboard. She is bought by a Boston family and educated by Nathaniel, one of the sons. She "performs" her poetry for important people in Boston, including John Hancock, and eventually travels to England where her poems are published. It is an exciting and challenging novel.

Time Enough for Drums (Random House, 1986) offers plenty of action, conspiracy, and adventure. Jemima Emerson is caught in the thorny conflict between England and the colonies. A dedicated rebel, Jemima gradually finds herself falling in love with her tutor, a staunch Tory loyal to the British.

A Ride into Morning: The Story of Tempe Wick (Harcourt, 1991) tells the story of Tempe Wick, a true heroine of the American Revolution. Tempe is a spoiled, stubborn girl living in a family that is threatened by the war. Told from the first-person point of view of her 14-year-old cousin Mary Cooper, the story details a soldier's mutiny in General Wayne's army and Tempe's role in the revolt against the atrocious conditions the soldiers endured.

The Second Bend in the River (Scholastic, 1997) is a unique love story between a pioneer girl named Rebecca Galloway and the great Shawnee chief Tecumseh. Told by Rebecca, the story offers remarkable insights into the relationships between white settlers and displaced Native Americans on the frontier in the early 1800s.

Other Books by Ann Rinaldi

A Break With Charity: A Story About the Salem Witch Trials. Harcourt, 1992.

Mine Eyes Have Seen. Scholastic, 1998.

Numbering All the Bones. Hyperion, 2002.

Taking Liberty: The Story of Oney Judge, George Washington's Runaway Slave. Simon & Schuster, 2002.

Wolf by the Ears. Scholastic, 1991.

The Serpent Never Sleeps

The Serpent Never Sleeps by Scott O'Dell is a novel set around the time of the early years of Jamestown. The heroine is Serena Lynn, a lady-in-waiting to a wealthy English countess. The book is Serena's first-person account of her attempt to save the life of the man she loves, the countess's son Anthony Foxglove, from a charge of murder. She details their sudden decision to emigrate to America. In the course of the voyage, they undergo Anthony's imprisonment and shipwreck on a deserted island in Bermuda.

The crew and passengers rebuild two ships and eventually sail to Jamestown, where they find the colony on the verge of total collapse after the Starving Time, a winter in which hundreds of settlers died. A new governor and the new settlers begin rebuilding the settlement. Serena becomes involved in the kidnapping of Pocahontas, and the two young women become friends during Pocahontas' captivity. Both girls acquire suitors who they eventually marry.

Assignment

Read *The Serpent Never Sleeps* by Scott O'Dell. Then answer the following questions on a separate sheet of paper.

1. What gift did King James give Serena?

2. Who is Anthony Foxglove's enemy?

3. What sport does King James enjoy?

4. What did John Smith do at the countess' party?

5. Who took Serena's ring?

6. Why was Anthony Foxglove locked up on board the *Sea Venture*?

7. What happened to *Gates' Gift*?

8. Why did the leaders of Jamestown kidnap Pocahontas?

9. What Indian couple helped kidnap Pocahontas?

10. Who fell in love with Pocahontas?

11. Who fell in love with Serena?

12. What did Serena do with the ring?

13. What happened to Anthony Foxglove?

14. Who does Serena adopt and care for?

15. What happened to Pocahontas?

1600	1650	1700	1750	1800	1850

The Serpent Never Sleeps (cont.)

Extension

Discuss the following questions with a small group or the entire class. Use evidence from *The Serpent Never Sleeps* to support your opinions.

1. Was Anthony Foxglove in love with Serena?

2. Describe the character and personality of King James.

3. Was Anthony Foxglove always going to have trouble with the authorities?

4. Did Pocahontas completely believe in the Christian religion?

5. Do you think Pocahontas was truly in love with John Rolfe?

6. Do you think Serena was in love with Tom Barlow?

7. Why did Serena go on the expedition to capture Pocahontas?

8. Was Sir Thomas Gates a good leader or a poor leader?

9. What were some of the problems Jamestown faced after Serena's arrival?

10. Why do you think Pocahontas's father did not send people to rescue her?

11. Who did not approve of the marriage of Pocahontas?

12. What kind of superstitious beliefs were common during this time period?

Other Books by Scott O'Dell

Alexandra. Houghton, 1984.

Island of the Blue Dolphins. Houghton, 1960.

My Name is Not Angelica. Dell, 1989.

Sarah Bishop. Scholastic, 1991.

Sing Down the Moon. Houghton, 1970.

Streams to the River, River to the Sea. Houghton, 1986.

Elements of a Story

Assignment

Read one of Ann Rinaldi's novels (listed on page 50) or one of the books written by Scott O'Dell (listed on page 52). Complete the outline below about the book. Then share the information with a small group or the entire class.

Story Outline

Genre (historical fiction, fantasy, contemporary realism): _____

Setting of the story (where and when): _____

Protagonist (one or two facts about the central character): _____

Major characters (include one or two descriptive facts about each): _____

_____

Lesser characters (include one or two descriptive facts about each): _____

_____

Point of view (Is the story told in first person or third person?): _____

Plot (3–6 sentences about the story line): _____

_____

_____

_____

_____

_____

Problem/Conflict (basic problem in one sentence): _____

_____

Climax (story's turning point): _____

_____

Resolution (how the story ends): _____

_____

Feeling/Tone (book's general tone—depressing, uplifting, sad, funny, etc.): _____

Theme (ideas the story addresses, such as good versus evil): _____

_____

Personal Evaluation (your response to the characters and story): _____

_____

_____

The Double Life of Pocahontas

The Double Life of Pocahontas by Jean Fritz is a spirited and fast-moving story of the life of Pocahontas. The author is deeply sensitive to Pocahontas's life and feelings as a Native American who moves uncomfortably between two cultures: her Indian family where her father is an important chief and the white English culture where she is sometimes respected but is usually treated as a pawn by the leaders of Jamestown and England. The story shows the conflict between Pocahontas' deep love for her father and her fascination with John Smith and the English settlers.

Assignment

Read *The Double Life of Pocahontas*, including the notes at the end of the book. Then answer the following questions on a separate sheet of paper.

1. What did Pocahontas do every morning when she arose?

2. How many settlers at Jamestown had died by the end of the first summer?

3. How did Pocahontas save John Smith's life in her father's longhouse?

4. What gift did John Smith agree to give to Powhatan that Rawhunt could not take home?

5. How was Pocahontas related to John Smith?

6. Why did John Smith return to England?

7. Why did Samuel Argall decide to kidnap Pocahontas?

8. Who was the cruelest governor of Jamestown?

9. What Indian couple helped Argall kidnap Pocahontas?

10. What English settler did Pocahontas marry?

11. Where did Pocahontas, her son, and her husband visit?

12. What did Powhatan want to know about England?

13. How did Pocahontas die?

14. How did the English treat Pocahontas?

15. What was John Smith's magic disk?

16. Who was John Rolfe?

The Double Life of Pocahontas *(cont.)*

Extension

Discuss the following questions with a small group or the entire class.

1. Do you think Pocahontas believed completely in Christianity?
2. Which religion seemed to give her more comfort—her Indian faith or Christian faith?
3. Was Pocahontas in love with John Smith or just intrigued by him?
4. Did Pocahontas love John Rolfe, or did she marry for other reasons?
5. Why did the leaders in England treat Pocahontas so well?
6. Why did England seem so different and strange to Pocahontas?
7. What did Pocahontas dislike about England?
8. Why did Pocahontas dread returning to Jamestown?
9. What should Powhatan and other leaders of the tribe have done about the settlement of Jamestown?
10. Who was the most admirable character in the book?
11. Which person did you like the least? Why?
12. How would you describe the character of John Smith? What were his strengths and weaknesses?

Assignment

Read one of the books written by Jean Fritz that is listed below, and make an oral report to the class about the book. Describe the main character, mention important details about his or her life, and tell about any interesting anecdotes or stories you read.

Books by Jean Fritz

And Then What Happened, Paul Revere? Putnam, 1973.
Bully for You, Teddy Roosevelt. Putnam, 1991.
Can't You Make Them Behave, King George? Putnam, 1996.
The Double Life of Pocahontas. Puffin, 1987.
George Washington's Mother. Putnam, 1992.
The Great Little Madison. Putnam, 1989.
Harriet Beecher Stowe and the Beecher Preachers. Putnam, 1994.
Just a Few Words, Mr. Lincoln. Stern Sloan, 1993.
Make Way for Sam Houston. Putnam, 1986.
Shh! We're Writing the Constitution. Putnam, 1997.
Traitor: The Case of Benedict Arnold. Puffin, 1989.
What's the Big Idea, Ben Franklin? Putnam, 1976.
Where Do You Think You're Going, Christopher Columbus? Putnam, 1981.
Where Was Patrick Henry on the 29th of May? Putnam, 1975.
Who's That Stepping on Plymouth Rock? Putnam, 1975.
Why Don't You Get a Horse, Sam Adams? Putnam, 1974.
Will You Sign Here, John Hancock? Putnam, 1976.
You Want Women to Vote, Lizzie Stanton? Putnam, 1995.

| 1600 | 1650 | 1700 | 1750 | 1800 | 1850 |

Readers' Theater Notes

Readers' Theater is drama without costumes, props, stage, or memorization. It can be done in the classroom by groups of students who become the cast of the dramatic reading.

Staging

Place four stools, chairs, or desks in a semicircle at the front of the classroom or in a separate stage area. Generally no costumes are used in this type of dramatization, but students dressed in similar clothing or colors can add a nice effect. Simple props can be used but are not required.

Script

Each member of the group should have a clearly marked script. Performers should practice several times before presenting the play to the class.

Performing

Performers should enter the classroom quietly and seriously. They should sit silently without moving and wait with heads lowered. The first reader should begin, and the other readers should focus on whoever is reading, except when they are performing.

Assignment

Read the Readers' Theater Script (pages 57 and 58) about the Starving Time in Jamestown. Work within the group to prepare for the performance.

Extension

Write your own Readers' Theater script based on one of the events listed below or another topic related to the colonial period. Practice your script with a group of classmates, and then perform it for the rest of the class.

- A slave makes the Middle Passage across the Atlantic.
- Roger Williams flees to Rhode Island.
- A witch is tried at the Salem witch trials.
- King Philip decides to attack Massachusetts settlers.
- Anne Hutchinson is banished from Massachusetts.
- The first slaves arrive in Jamestown.
- An English fleet captures New Amsterdam.
- The first Thanksgiving is held in Plymouth.
- William Penn establishes Philadelphia.

Readers' Theater: The Starving Time

The following script is a fictional account of a meeting at the end of the terrible winter of 1609–1610 when the settlement of Jamestown came close to total failure.

Narrator: The time is May 1610 in Jamestown, Virginia, after a terrible winter which fewer than 60 settlers out of 500 have survived. The settlement had been on the edge of survival since it was founded in the spring of 1607. Most of the settlers were spoiled gentlemen adventurers who were not prepared by personality or training for a life of extreme physical labor and hardship. Only a few hard-working farmers, some servants, and an occasional craftsman were scattered among the gentlemen. Sir Thomas Gates, the new governor, has just arrived in the settlement, which is in ruins. He joins three men who are sitting in the ruins of a house. Captain George Percy is the acting governor. Reverend Waite and John Laydon, a carpenter, are the other two.

Sir Thomas Gates: We have just arrived from England. Our ship was wrecked in a hurricane near Bermuda, and we had to spend several months there building two small vessels to get us here. This is not the settlement I expected. We heard that Jamestown was becoming prosperous. What has happened?

Reverend Waite: This has been a winter of terror and terrible sadness. I feel at times that we have been abandoned by God. We spend most of our time burying our dead. We are almost too weak to do a decent Christian job of it. We barely get them beneath the earth and say a few prayers.

John Laydon: At least they are mostly buried. One poor man slew his own wife when she was near death and started eating her. He is not the only one here to go raving mad either. We are grateful to see you, Governor, but we have nothing to offer you. I hope you brought food. Our people are starving to death.

Captain Percy: We have had a terrible time. The winter has been bitter cold. So many men were ill that many of the houses and parts of the fortification have been used for firewood. This has been especially troublesome because the savage Indians have determined to destroy us. We cannot go outside the settlement without being attacked by a swarm of arrows fired from a dozen different hiding places.

John Laydon: Jamestown was a terrible place for a settlement in the first place. It is not easy to defend, and the chief of the local Indian tribe has determined to destroy us. When Captain Smith was here, we often were able to trade with the Indians for corn and other food but no longer.

Readers' Theater: The Starving Time *(cont.)*

Sir Thomas Gates: Where are all the gold and riches we were told about?

Reverend Waite: The gold is in the fool heads of the investors in England and our own gentlemen. They spent the entire summer last year digging up fool's gold and looking for gems and riches. It was the only work those worthless gentlemen did.

John Laydon: It was different when John Smith was governor. He made the rule, "If you do not work, you do not eat," and he enforced this rule.

Captain Percy: I took over when Captain Smith was wounded and left for England in October. We thought there was plenty of food in the settlement and easy hunting in the forests, but the Indians killed many of our hunters. The corn was quickly devoured, some of it by rats. Wild pigs and birds are in the forest, but we cannot get to them.

Reverend Waite: We have had terrible sicknesses, too. This land is swampy. The water is bad and often not fit for drinking. We have had typhoid fever, dysentery, and all other manner of illness. Most of the women and children here have died.

John Laydon: We have eaten everything we could. You will notice there are no dogs or cats. They have long since been in the cook pots. We have eaten every form of snake and creature that has been unlucky enough to be seen. The few pigs and hens that were in the settlement were eaten by the gentlemen. They were not inclined to share either.

Reverend Waite: Many of us have eaten our boots and shoes, as you can plainly see. Our people are nearly as barefoot as the Indians.

Captain Percy: We do not even know what happened to some of our residents. Desperate for food, they went outside the fort and never returned— either killed or captured by the natives. I do not know which would be worse. What shall we do?

Sir Thomas Gates: I do not see any choice but to return to England. We can load your survivors onto our two boats and hope we make it back to England.

Narrator: That is exactly what was done. On June 7, 1610, the settlers climbed aboard ship and set off for England. They sailed only a short distance before encountering a fleet of ships carrying 300 more settlers and a new governor. They returned to Jamestown, and this time they stuck it out.

1600   1650   1700   1750   1800   1850

Teacher Lesson Plans for Social Studies

Using Time Lines

Objectives: Students will learn to derive information from a time line and create time lines that are relevant to them.

Materials: copies of Colonial Time Line (pages 61 and 62); research resources including books, encyclopedias, texts, atlases, almanacs, and Internet sites

Procedure

1. Collect available resources for students so that they have plenty of reference materials.

2. Reproduce and distribute the Colonial Time Line activity sheet (pages 61 and 62). Review the various events listed on the time line.

3. Have students place additional dates on the time line as described in the assignment on page 62. Inform students that they may also use the readings from previous lessons to find extra dates to include on the time line.

4. If desired, have students create their own personal time lines as described in the extension activity at the bottom of page 62.

Assessment: Have students share their additions to the time line, using the board or a chart to list the new dates and events. Allow students to share their personal time lines in groups or with the class.

Using Maps

Objective: Students will learn to use and derive information from a variety of maps.

Materials: copies of Triangle Trade Maps (page 63); copies of Map of the Colonies in 1733 (page 64); copies of Map of the Colonies in 1763 (page 65); atlases, almanacs, and other maps for reference and comparison

Procedure

1. Review the Triangle Trade Maps (page 63) activity sheet with students. Point out important features of the maps. Instruct students to answer the questions at the bottom of the page independently.

2. Review the Map of the Colonies in 1733 (page 64) activity sheet with students. Have them use the map to complete the activity.

3. Review the Map of the Colonies in 1763 (page 65) activity sheet with students. Have them complete the map as instructed on the page.

Assessment: Correct the map activity pages with the students. Check for understanding and review basic concepts.

Teacher Lesson Plans for Social Studies *(cont.)*

Researching Colonial Life, Events, and People

Objectives: Students will develop skills in finding, organizing, and presenting research information.

Materials: copies of Researching Colonial Life, Events, and People (pages 66 and 67); copies of Colonial Men and Women (page 68); books, encyclopedias, and Internet sources

Procedure

1. Reproduce and distribute copies of Researching Colonial Life, Events, and People (pages 66 and 67) and Colonial Men and Women (page 68). Inform students that they will be writing a report about the colonies. Review the Writing a Report guidelines (page 66). Discuss the assignment, and then let students choose a topic.

2. Discuss potential sources to use, the need to take notes in an organized manner, and what kind of information is required. (*Multimedia Collections: Colonial America*, TCM3035, contains a variety of relevant clip art, photographs, documents, and video and audio clips that can be used to enhance reports or presentations.)

3. Give students time to prepare their reports. Allow them opportunities to use the school library and classroom reference materials as needed.

4. Have students share their reports with the class. Encourage them to bring visuals or illustrations to make their presentation more engaging.

Assessment: Assess students on the basis of their written reports and oral classroom presentations.

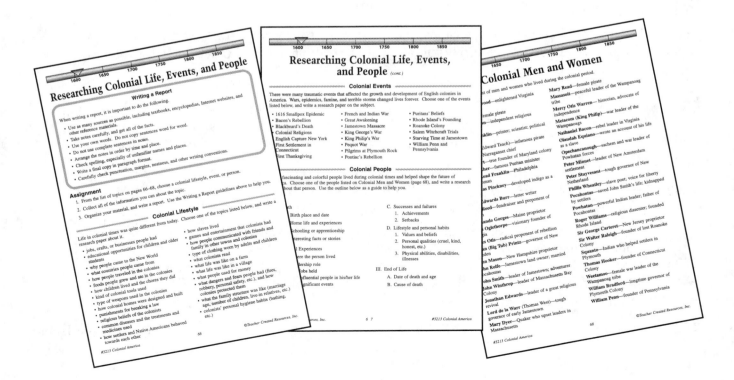

Colonial Time Line

1492—Christopher Columbus discovers America.

1565—The first permanent colony in present-day United States is founded by the Spanish at St. Augustine, Florida.

1585—Sir Walter Raleigh establishes the first English colony in North America at Roanoke, Virginia. It does not survive.

1607—The first permanent English settlement in North America is founded at Jamestown, Virginia. Pocahontas saves John Smith's life.

1609—Henry Hudson explores the Hudson River.
Virginians begin growing tobacco as a cash crop.
About 440 of 500 Jamestown residents die during a winter of starvation.

1613—Pocahontas is kidnapped by Jamestown colonists.

1614—Pocahontas marries John Rolfe in Jamestown.

1616—Smallpox epidemic destroys most of the Indian tribes from Maine to Rhode Island.

1617—Pocahontas dies of smallpox in England.

1619—The first African slaves arrive in Virginia.
The first legislative assembly in the English colonies, the House of Burgesses, convenes in Virginia.

1620—Pilgrims arrive on the Mayflower and found Plymouth Colony, Massachusetts.

1622—Jamestown's conflict with powerful neighboring Indian tribes leads to massacres of white settlers and Indians.

1624—The Dutch begin settling New Netherlands.

1626—Dutch West India Company buys Manhattan Island from the Indians.

1627—About 1,500 kidnapped children arrive in Virginia from England to help populate the colony.

1629—About 900 Puritans led by John Winthrop found Massachusetts Bay Colony.

1630—John Winthrop establishes the town of Boston.

1632—Lord Baltimore founds the colony of Maryland.

1634—A smallpox epidemic kills more than 90 per cent of Indians living in the Connecticut River Valley.

1636—Roger Williams establishes a colony in Rhode Island open to diverse religious groups.
Thomas Hooker leads settlers establishing colony in Connecticut.
Harvard College is founded in Massachusetts.

1637—Religious dissenter Anne Hutchinson flees from the Massachusetts Bay Colony to Rhode Island.
The colony of New Sweden is founded in what is now Delaware.

Colonial Time Line *(cont.)*

1647—Massachusetts requires public schools in most settlements.

1652—Rhode Island enacts the first law in the colonies banning slavery.

1663—Carolina is founded.

1664—The English capture New Amsterdam and rename it New York.
The Duke of York creates New Jersey from his New York property.

1670—Charleston is founded in South Carolina.

1675—King Philip's War between colonists and Indians leads to massacres on both sides.

1676—Bacon's Rebellion against the Virginia government destroys much of Jamestown.

1679—New Hampshire is founded.

1681—William Penn founds Pennsylvania as a Quaker colony.

1701—Delaware becomes independent of Pennsylvania.

1704—The Boston News-Letter becomes the first successful newspaper in the British colonies.

1706—Ben Franklin is born in Boston, Massachusetts.

1730—North and South Carolina split into two royal colonies.

1732—Georgia is founded as a haven for debtors by James Oglethorpe.
Ben Franklin begins publishing *Poor Richard's Almanac.*

1734—The Great Awakening, a widespread religious revival, spreads through the colonies.

1752—Ben Franklin performs his famous kite experiment.

1754—The French and Indian War between France and Britain begins.

1763—The French and Indian War ends with British control of eastern North America.

Assignment

1. Find at least 10 dates in American history before 1800 to add to the Colonial Time Line. These dates could include wars, inventions, disasters, birth dates of colonial leaders, or other events. Use textbooks, encyclopedias, and Internet searches to find events and dates.

2. Make a list of these dates in chronological (time) order to share with the class. Be sure to include brief background information about each of these additional dates.

Extension

1. Make a time line with 10 important world events that have occurred in your lifetime.

2. Then add 10 dates of important events in your own life to the time line.

3. Share your time line with a small group or the entire class.

Triangle Trade Maps

The maps below illustrate two versions of the triangle trade which colonists conducted. Both trade patterns involved slaves.

Assignment

Use the maps to answer the following questions.

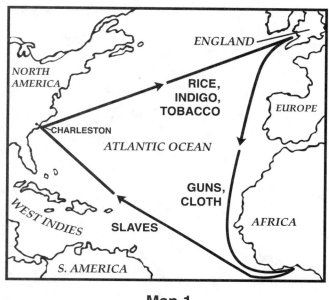

Map 1   **Map 2**

Map 1

1. What was the destination of a ship leaving Charleston? _____

2. What did a ship leaving Charleston carry? _____

3. What did a ship carry from Africa to Charleston? _____

4. What did a ship carry from England to Africa? _____

Map 2

5. What was the destination of a ship leaving Boston? _____

6. What did a ship leaving Boston carry? _____

7. What did a ship carry from Africa to the West Indies? _____

8. What did a ship carry from the West Indies back to Boston? _____

9. What ocean did all these ships cross? _____

10. What three continents were involved in this trade? _____

Map of the Colonies 1733

The map here shows the British colonies in America.

Assignment

Read page 14, and then list each of the colonies below.

New England Colonies

1. _____
2. _____
3. _____
4. _____

Middle Colonies

1. _____
2. _____
3. _____
4. _____

Southern Colonies

1. _____
2. _____
3. _____
4. _____
5. _____

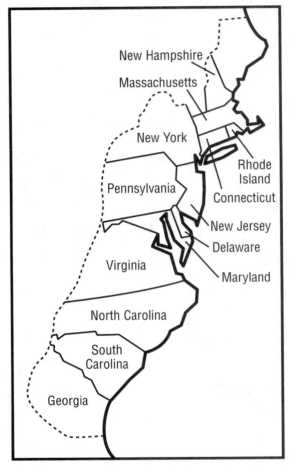

Extension

Read pages 8–13. Then list in order from earliest to most recent the 13 colonies and the year each was founded.

	Colony	Year Founded
1.	_____	_____
2.	_____	_____
3.	_____	_____
4.	_____	_____
5.	_____	_____
6.	_____	_____
7.	_____	_____
8.	_____	_____
9.	_____	_____
10.	_____	_____
11.	_____	_____
12.	_____	_____
13.	_____	_____

1600 1650 1700 1750 1800 1850

Map of the Colonies in 1763

Directions: On the map below, label the British colonies in 1763. Use colored pencils or crayons to indicate which were the New England, Middle, and Southern colonies. Add the following major cities to the map, and label and color the bodies of water. Use an atlas or almanac to help you.

Colonies

Connecticut
Delaware
Georgia
Maryland
Massachusetts
New Hampshire
New Jersey
New York
North Carolina
Pennsylvania
Rhode Island
South Carolina
Virginia

Cities

Baltimore, MD
Boston, MA
Charleston, SC
Hartford, CT
Jamestown, VA
New York City, NY
Philadelphia, PA
Plymouth, MA
Salem, MA
Savannah, GA

Bodies of Water

Atlantic Ocean
Chesapeake Bay

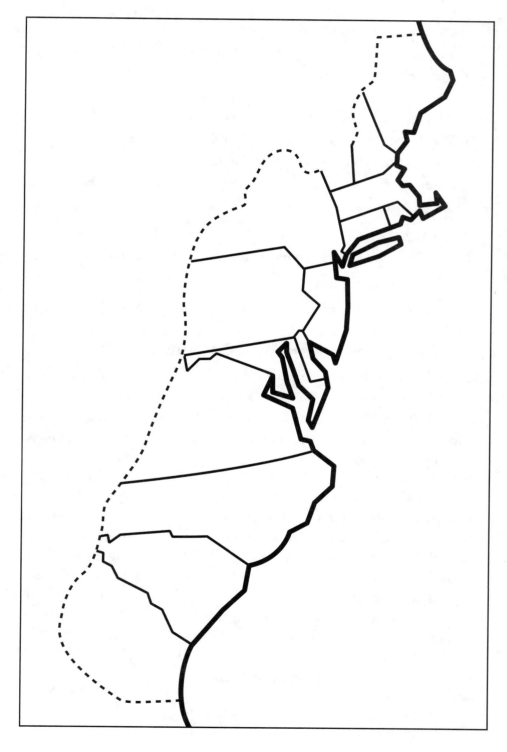

1600   **1650**   **1700**   **1750**   **1800**   **1850**

Researching Colonial Life, Events, and People

Writing a Report

When writing a report, it is important to do the following.

- Use as many sources as possible, including textbooks, encyclopedias, Internet websites, and other reference materials.
- Take notes carefully, and get all of the facts.
- Use your own words. Do not copy sentences word for word.
- Do not use complete sentences in notes.
- Arrange the notes in order by time and place.
- Check spelling, especially of unfamiliar names and places.
- Write a final copy in paragraph format.
- Carefully check punctuation, margins, neatness, and other writing conventions.

Assignment

1. From the list of topics on pages 66–68, choose a colonial lifestyle, event, or person.

2. Collect all of the information you can about the topic.

3. Organize your material, and write a report. Use the Writing a Report guidelines above to help you.

Colonial Lifestyle

Life in colonial times was quite different from today. Choose one of the topics listed below, and write a research paper about it.

- jobs, crafts, or businesses people had
- educational opportunities for children and older students
- why people came to the New World
- what countries people came from
- how people traveled in the colonies
- foods people grew and ate in the colonies
- how children lived and the chores they did
- kind of colonial tools used
- type of weapons used in the colonies
- how colonial homes were designed and built
- punishments for breaking a law
- religious beliefs of the colonists
- common diseases and the treatments and medicines used
- how settlers and Native Americans behaved towards each other

- how slaves lived
- games and entertainment that colonists had
- how people communicated with friends and family in other towns and colonies
- type of clothing worn by adults and children
- what colonists read
- what life was like on a farm
- what life was like in a village
- what people used for money
- what dangers and fears people had (fires, robbery, personal safety, etc.), and how colonies protected them
- what the family structure was like (marriage age, number of children, live-in relatives, etc.)
- colonists' personal hygiene habits (bathing, etc.)

Researching Colonial Life, Events, and People *(cont.)*

Colonial Events

There were many traumatic events that affected the growth and development of English colonies in America. Wars, epidemics, famine, and terrible storms changed lives forever. Choose one of the events listed below, and write a research paper on the subject.

- 1616 Smallpox Epidemic
- Bacon's Rebellion
- Blackbeard's Death
- Colonial Religions
- English Capture New York
- First Settlement in Connecticut
- First Thanksgiving

- French and Indian War
- Great Awakening
- Jamestown Massacre
- King George's War
- King Philip's War
- Pequot War
- Pilgrims at Plymouth Rock
- Pontiac's Rebellion

- Puritans' Beliefs
- Rhode Island's Founding
- Roanoke Colony
- Salem Witchcraft Trials
- Starving Time at Jamestown
- William Penn and Pennsylvania

Colonial People

Many fascinating and colorful people lived during colonial times and helped shape the future of America. Choose one of the people listed on Colonial Men and Women (page 68), and write a research paper about that person. Use the outline below as a guide to help you.

I. Youth

    A. Birth place and date

    B. Home life and experiences

    C. Schooling or apprenticeship

    D. Interesting facts or stories

II. Colonial Experiences

    A. Where the person lived

    B. Leadership role

        1. Jobs held

        2. Influential people in his/her life

        3. Significant events

    C. Successes and failures

        1. Achievements

        2. Setbacks

    D. Lifestyle and personal habits

        1. Values and beliefs

        2. Personal qualities (cruel, kind, honest, etc.)

        3. Physical abilities, disabilities, illnesses

III. End of Life

    A. Date of death and age

    B. Cause of death

Colonial Men and Women

Below is a partial list of men and women who lived during the colonial period.

Alexander Spotswood—enlightened Virginia governor

Anne Bonney—female pirate

Anne Hutchinson—independent religious dissenter

Benjamin Franklin—printer; scientist; political leader

Blackbeard (Edward Teach)—infamous pirate

Canonicus—Narraganset chief

Cecil Calvert—true founder of Maryland colony

Cotton Mather—famous Puritan minister

Deborah Read Franklin—Philadelphia businesswoman

Eliza Lucas Pinckney—developed indigo as a cash crop

Esther Edwards Burr—letter writer

Esther Reed—fundraiser and proponent of freedom

Ferdinando Gorges—Maine proprietor

James Oglethorpe—visionary founder of Georgia

James Otis—radical proponent of rebellion

Johan (Big Tub) Printz—governor of New Sweden

John Mason—New Hampshire proprietor

John Rolfe—Jamestown land owner; married Pocahontas

John Smith—leader of Jamestown; adventurer

John Winthrop—leader of Massachusetts Bay Colony

Jonathan Edwards—leader of a great religious revival

Lord de la Warr (Thomas West)—tough governor of early Jamestown

Mary Dyer—Quaker who upset leaders in Massachusetts

Mary Read—female pirate

Massasoit—peaceful leader of the Wampanoag tribe

Mercy Otis Warren— historian, advocate of independence

Metacom (King Philip)—war leader of the Wampanoags

Nathaniel Bacon—rebel leader in Virginia

Olaudah Equiano—wrote an account of his life as a slave

Opechancanough—sachem and war leader of Powhatan forces

Peter Minuet—leader of New Amsterdam settlement

Peter Stuyvesant—tough governor of New Netherland

Phillis Wheatley—slave poet; voice for liberty

Pocahontas—saved John Smith's life; kidnapped by settlers

Powhatan—powerful Indian leader; father of Pocahontas

Roger Williams—religious dissenter; founded Rhode Island

Sir George Carteret—New Jersey proprietor

Sir Walter Raleigh—founder of lost Roanoke Colony

Squanto—Indian who helped settlers in Plymouth

Thomas Hooker—founder of Connecticut Colony

Weetamoo—female war leader of the Wampanoag tribe

William Bradford—longtime governor of Plymouth Colony

William Penn—founder of Pennsylvania

Teacher Lesson Plans for Science and Physical Education

Colonial Science

Objective: Students will replicate simple science projects related to colonial days.

Materials: copies of Pinwheels (page 70); copies of Wind Wheels (page 71); copies of Growing Plants (page 72); copies of Plant Growth Sheet (page 73); science materials listed on each page including paper, ruler, scissors, tape, straight pins, pencils, large straws, thin straws, index cards, lima beans, corn kernels, potting soil, Styrofoam cups, sealable plastic bags, paper towels, water

Procedure

1. Collect the materials listed on each page before assigning each project.

2. Reproduce and distribute the Pinwheels activity sheet (page 70). Review the information, distribute the materials, and read the directions for making and using the pinwheel.

3. Reproduce and distribute the Wind Wheels activity sheet (page 71). Review the information, distribute the materials, and read the directions for making and using the wind wheels.

4. Reproduce and distribute the Succotash experiment (page 72). Review the information, distribute the materials, and read the directions for growing the seeds in soil.

5. Reproduce and distribute the Hydroponic Succotash experiment (page 72) and Plant Growth Sheet (page 73). Review the information, distribute the materials, and read the directions for growing the seeds in water. Have students observe, record, and sketch the seeds daily for about 10 days. If desired, allow students to work with a partner.

Assessment: Have students share their wind wheel designs and planting experiences with the class in a scientific colloquium in which students ask questions and relate their experiences to classmates.

Colonial Games and Sports

Objectives: Students will discover the historical roots of many of their games and replicate them with modern materials.

Materials: copies of Colonial Games and Sports (page 74) and available materials as indicated in the text

Procedure

1. Reproduce and distribute the Colonial Games and Sports activity sheet (page 74).

2. Review the information, help students brainstorm ideas for playing games in a modern context, and suggest possible materials.

Assessment: Have students share their experiences in a discussion after their games.

Pinwheels

The colonists were very concerned about wind because it had such a strong effect on their lives. The wind could cause terrible damage, but it also powered windmills and sailing ships. Windmills were common throughout the colonies, especially in New Amsterdam (New York). They were usually used to grind grain into flour.

Making a Pinwheel

Pinwheels are air powered. Follow the directions below to make a simple pinwheel.

Materials: paper, ruler, scissors, tape, straight pin or push pin, pencil or straw

Procedure

1. Use a ruler to measure a piece of paper 5 inches square.

2. Cut out the 5-inch square, and draw two diagonal lines across the square.

3. On the diagonal lines, measure and cut 2½ inches from each corner.

4. Fold one corner into the middle. Tape it down so that a loop of paper is formed as shown in the illustration.

5. Skip the other cut corner in that quadrant. Fold the first corner to make a loop in the next quadrant, and tape it down.

6. Follow the same pattern with the remaining two corners.

7. Push a straight pin or push pin through the center of the wheel and into a pencil eraser or a straw.

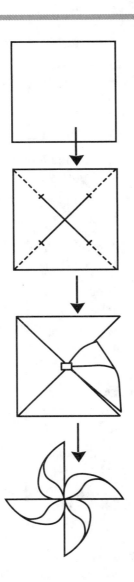

Using the Pinwheel

Test out the pinwheel you made. Blow gently on it. Then blow harder. How fast can you make it whirl?

Go outside and position the wheel so that the wind catches the loops of the wheel. Run with the wheel to create a moving stream of air hitting the loops. Which system made the wheel go fastest?

Wind Wheels

Making a Mini-Wheel

Follow the directions below to make a miniature pinwheel.

Materials: index card, ruler, scissors, tape, straight pin or push pin, pencil or straw

Procedure

1. Cut a 3-inch square from an index card, and draw diagonal lines from corner to corner.

2. On the diagonal lines, cut 1½ inches from each corner.

3. Fold one corner into the middle. Tape it down so that a loop of paper is formed as shown in the illustration.

4. Skip the other cut corner in that quadrant. Fold the first corner to make a loop in the next quadrant, and tape it down.

5. Follow the same pattern with the remaining two corners.

6. Push a straight pin or push pin through the center of the wheel and into a pencil eraser or a straw.

Using the Mini-Wheel

Test the wheel. Does it whirl faster or slower? Why would smaller wheels sometimes be easier to work? Do they always catch the wind as well?

Making a Double Wind Wheel

Use the pinwheel (page 70) you made previously and the mini-wheel you made above to create a double wind wheel.

Materials: scissors, tape, straight pin, thin straw, larger straw

Procedure

1. Slit both ends of a thin straw about 1 inch along each end.

2. Flatten the ends against the outside of one of the wheels, and tape the wheel to the straw.

3. Cut a larger straw about 2 or 3 inches shorter than the thin straw, and thread the wider straw over the thinner straw.

4. Tape the other end of the thin straw to the other wheel. Make sure the loops or folds on each wheel are facing the same way into the wind.

Using the Double Wind Wheel

Hold the double wind wheel by the large straw in the center. Face into the wind and watch both wheels turn. Why is it a little harder to get the double wheel to work? Does the double wheel work when you blow on it? Does it work when you run with it? Tape the large center straw to a pole or anywhere it can move freely, and observe the double wind wheel. How does it compare to the pinwheel you made?

Growing Plants

Succotash

Squanto taught the Pilgrims how to plant beans and corn together in a mound with three or four seeds and the inedible remains of a fish, which served as fertilizer. Colonists often cooked lima beans and corn together in a dish they called *succotash*.

Growing Seeds in Soil

Materials: 3 lima beans (packaged, dry beans will work), 3 corn kernels, Styrofoam cup, potting soil, water, tray or plate

Procedure

1. Punch four holes in the bottom of a Styrofoam cup to allow drainage.

2. Fill the Styrofoam cup with loose potting soil.

3. Plant the three lima beans and three corn kernels and cover with about ½ inch of soil.

4. Slowly water with about one ounce of water. Some water will drain out so keep the cups in a tray or plate.

5. The plants may be kept inside or outside, but the temperature should be moderate.

6. Water as needed (about every other day).

7. Observe the growth of your plants. Compare how well these plants grow over the same time period to those grown in water (see the Hydroponic Succotash experiment below).

8. Plant the entire cup in a garden when the plants are about 3 inches high. For best results, keep only the strongest corn plant and the strongest bean plant. Pull out the weaker plants.

Hydroponic Succotash

Hydroponic growing uses water—but no dirt—to grow plants. In this experiment you will be able to see how each plant develops.

Growing Seeds in Water

Materials: sealable quart-size plastic bags, 3 lima beans, 3 corn kernels, paper towel, water

Procedure

1. Fold a paper towel, and place it in a plastic bag that seals at the top.

2. Slowly pour about one ounce of water over the towel. The towel should be damp but not soaked and dripping.

3. Carefully place 3 lima beans and 3 corn kernels in a row on the paper towel in the bag.

4. Seal the bag.

5. Observe the growth of your plants. Measure the height of the plants and record the measurements on the Plant Growth Sheet (page 73). Compare how well these plants grow to those grown in soil (see the Succotash experiment above).

Plant Growth Sheet

Examine your seeds daily. Measure each stem and root as it grows, and record your observations on this sheet. On the right-hand side, draw pictures showing the seeds' growth.

Plant Growth Record

Day 1

Bean observations: _____

Corn observations: _____

Day 2

Bean observations: _____

Corn observations: _____

Day 3

Bean observations: _____

Corn observations: _____

Day 4

Bean observations: _____

Corn observations: _____

Day 5

Bean observations: _____

Corn observations: _____

Day 6

Bean observations: _____

Corn observations: _____

Day 7

Bean observations: _____

Corn observations: _____

Day 8

Bean observations: _____

Corn observations: _____

Day 9

Bean observations: _____

Corn observations: _____

Day 10

Bean observations: _____

Corn observations: _____

Extension

Turn your bag upside down, and leave it for a few days. What happened to the stem and the roots?

Colonial Games and Sports

Choose one of the games or sports listed below to play during your next physical education or recess period.

Rolling Hoops

Round metal hoops used to surround wooden barrels, and the rims of wagon wheels were often used for races. You can use hula-hoops for the same purpose. Choose a starting line, and race a friend while rolling your hoop. These can be one-on-one races or races with many contestants.

Quoits

All you need are some rings about the diameter of a plate and some stakes. You can use croquet stakes, pieces of doweling, or even paper towel tubes stuck in the ground for the stakes. The rings could be cutout paper plates, bands of tagboard made into a circle and stapled, or similar objects. The object of the game is to successfully throw a ring over the stake. Start at a distance of four feet from the stake and keep lengthening the distance to see how well you can do. This game works well with two to four players.

Walking on Stilts

Walking on stilts was popular in colonial times and in most periods until recent times. Colonial children used whatever pieces of wood they could find. You can make a modified pair of stilts by using large soup or fruit drink cans or even full toilet paper rolls. Use masking tape or duct tape to attach the stilts to your shoes. Use two, long, sturdy poles to help you keep your balance.

Marbles

Marbles have been popular since colonial times. Draw a circle in the dirt or on the pavement about the size of a hula-hoop. Place one marble inside the circle. Take turns trying to hit that marble by rolling a marble from outside the circle. If you miss, your marble stays in the circle. The person who hits the center marble wins all the marbles left in the circle.

Familiar Games

Hopscotch was called "Scotch-hoppers" in colonial times, but the rules were about the same as they are today. Back then children would have marked their playing area in the dirt. Children played both chess and checkers. They also played with tops, whistles, kites, dollhouses, and snow sleds. Tag, foot races, sack races, and Blind Man's Bluff were popular, too.

Culminating Activities for Colonial Day

Colonial Day

Set aside one day to be devoted to activities related to your study of colonial life. If possible, do this with two or three classes at the same grade level. This allows you to share some of the responsibilities and provides a special experience for the entire grade level.

Costumes

Invite students to come in period costumes that look like the colonial era. Encourage them to find leather shoes, boots, or moccasins instead of tennis shoes. Ask one or two mothers to use makeup to provide some mustaches and beards for boys to give them a period look for the day. Encyclopedias, books about colonial life, and Internet websites offer many illustrations for students to copy and use.

Long socks pulled over pants will work well as will a white dress shirt and a man's dark suit coat. A handkerchief or piece of lace fabric can be used for the ruffles at the neck. Black construction paper can be used for pilgrim hats. Long dresses will work for the girls.

Parent Help

Encourage parents or adult family members to come for all or part of the day to enjoy the proceedings and also help set up and monitor the activities. Check with parents to discover any special talents, interests, or hobbies that would be a match for specific centers.

Eat Hearty

If you have parent volunteers, plan a luncheon with a colonial theme. Have students make decorations at one of the centers. Most modern children are far more picky than their colonial counterparts, but you might choose some dishes, such as succotash, with a colonial flavor.

Setting Up Centers

The centers you set up should relate in some way to the colonial period, daily life during that time, or activities you did using this book. Centers should involve small groups of six or seven students doing an activity and/or making something they can put on display. Each center should take about 20 minutes, after which time students should rotate to the next activity.

The following suggestions will get you started. You can add any others for which you have special expertise.

❑ **Readers' Theater**

In this center students could practice with a script for a readers' theater presentation. The script could be the one in this book (pages 57 and 58) or one that students have written based on a colonial event or story (see the Extension activity on page 56), such as the first Thanksgiving, the massacre at Jamestown, the capture of New York, or the Salem witch trials.

Culminating Activities for Colonial Day *(cont.)*

Setting Up Centers *(cont.)*

☐ **Reconstructing Colonial Homes and Villages**

Students at this center could build colonial homes, farms, and buildings out of modeling clay, craft sticks, twigs, small pieces of fabric, construction paper, and other resources. Provide pictures of various structures from several colonies, and allow students to arrange the buildings into villages.

☐ **Indian Homes and Villages**

Students could construct Iroquois longhouses plus tools, weapons, and artifacts used in an Iroquois village, or they could build the wigwams and thatched houses of the Algonquian peoples. Provide pictures of these types of homes as well as supplies like twigs, craft sticks, modeling clay, etc.

☐ **Building Forts**

Students working at this center could construct the fort at Jamestown and the surrounding villages. Students could expand on the work of each previous group.

☐ **Colonial Games**

Colonial games included foot races, variations of hide-and-seek, rolling hoops, flying kites, and Blindman's Bluff. Toys included tops and marbles. A sports center could feature relay races, sack races, and one-on-one contests between students. Toys and games could occupy a second center. Use page 74 for other ideas for these centers.

☐ **Map Making**

A variety of maps could be created at this center. Use the map section of this book for examples, and find others in atlases, encyclopedias, and the Internet. Small groups of two or three students could create these maps on tagboard, large construction paper, or in three-dimensional form using clay or salt and flour.

☐ **Model Boats**

One center could be devoted to making a model sailing ship like those used to bring colonists from England. Students could also build a ship showing how slaves were brought to America. Use Styrofoam trays for the hull and craft sticks, pipe cleaners, and other materials for the masts.

☐ **Clay Sculptures or Busts**

Students could use modeling or sculpting clay to make figures or busts of colonial characters they have studied. A 25-pound bag of sculpting clay can be divided into 18 or more rectangular blocks of clay with a piece of fishing line. Use toothpicks, craft sticks, or plastic knives to carve the features. Have paper towels available for cleanup.

☐ **Other Centers**

Other centers could include learning a square dance, weaving a simple pattern with yarn, tying knots, or an easy woodworking project.

Annotated Bibliography

Nonfiction

Carlson, Laurie. *Colonial Kids: An Activity Guide to Life in the New World*. Chicago Review Press, 1997. (Great idea book for activities with a colonial flavor)

Day, Nancy. *Your Travel Guide to Colonial America*. Lerner, 2001. (Intriguing account of life in the colonies from a tourist's point of view)

Fisher, Leonard Everett. *Colonial Craftsmen: The Schoolmasters*. Marshall Cavendish, 1997. (One of a series of classic accounts of the life and work of various colonial craftsmen, including silversmiths, doctors, glassmakers, and others)

Hakim, Joy. *Making Thirteen Colonies*. Oxford University Press, 1993. (Detailed, vivid account of colonial development with anecdotes)

Haskins, James and Kathleen Benson. *Bound For America: The Forced Migration of Africans to the New World*. Lothrop, Lee & Shepard, 1999. (Superbly illustrated account of the slave trade, especially the ocean voyage)

Kent, Deborah. *How We Lived . . . In the Middle Colonies*. Marshall Cavendish, 2000. (A three-book series—one for each geographic area—with a good account of daily life in the colonies)

King, David C. *Colonial Days*. Wiley, 1998. (Projects, games, and other activities related to colonial days)

Leon, Vicki. *Uppity Women of the New World*. Barnes & Noble, 2001. (Vignettes of interesting women who lived during the colonial era and early national period)

Maestro, Betsy. *Struggle for a Continent: The French and Indian Wars 1689–1763*. HarperCollins, 2000. (Superbly illustrated, easy-to-read account of the century of warfare between the superpowers of the time—England and France)

Roberts, Cokie. *Founding Mothers: The Women Who Raised Our Nation*. HarperCollins, 2004. (A well-written look at early American history from a female perspective)

Stefoff, Rebecca. *The Colonies*. Marshall Cavendish, 2001. (A brief but excellent account of colonial development)

Steins, Richard. *Colonial America*. Steck-Vaughn, 2000. (Solid account of colonial life by geographical area)

Other

Multimedia Collections: Colonial America. TCR3035. 2001. (A variety of relevant clip art, photographs, documents, and video clips, music, and sound effects to enhance reports or presentations)

Picture Books

Coleman, Brooke and Susan Whitehurst. *The Library of the Thirteen Colonies and the Lost Colony*. Rosen Publishing Group, 2000. (A series of 14 books with brief historical accounts of each colony's creation and early development)

Glossary

agriculture—farming; growing crops and raising livestock

apprentice—a person who learns a trade from a master craftsman

Burgesses—elected lawmakers in Virginia

cash crop—a crop grown to sell or export, such as tobacco

charter—an official document giving a colony the right to exist

Church of England—church created by King Henry VIII in 1534

colony—a territory owned by another nation

debtor—a person who owes money

dissident—a person who disagrees with laws or practices

Dutch—people from Holland (the Netherlands)

forgery—falsifying a document or currency

found (a colony)—to start a colony and support its growth

hornbook—flat, wooden board with a prayer or the alphabet protected by a translucent piece of thin cow horn

indenture—a contract binding someone to be a servant to another for a period of years

indigo—a plant which makes a bright blue dye

lords proprietors—wealthy noblemen who received large land grants from the king

massacre—the killing of many people

Middle Passage—the transatlantic journey for slaves from Africa to America

molasses—a dark, sweet syrup made from sugarcane

Pilgrims—English religious dissidents who wanted to separate from the official Church of England

plantation—a large farm which grew one or two main crops

plunder—to steal and destroy

population—the number of people living in a geographic area

primer—book used to teach young people to read

Protestant—a non-Catholic Christian

perjury—testifying to something known to be untrue

Puritans—English religious dissidents who wanted to purify and reform the official Church of England

Quaker—member of the Society of Friends who were opposed to war and slavery

sachem—an Indian wise man and chief

shackle—metal cuff used to chain hands and feet

smallpox—very contagious, deadly disease which leaves blisters or pockmarks on survivors; very common in colonial times

toleration—to be accepting of different races and religions

witchcraft—use of sorcery or magic or being accused of it

Answer Key

Page 33

1. b
2. a
3. b
4. c
5. b
6. b
7. c
8. a
9. b
10. d

Page 34

1. d
2. b
3. c
4. c
5. b
6. a
7. b
8. a
9. a
10. c

Page 35

1. b
2. d
3. a
4. c
5. c
6. a
7. d
8. c
9. c
10. b

Page 36

1. a
2. b
3. d
4. c
5. c
6. d
7. b
8. a
9. b
10. c

Page 37

1. b
2. c
3. c
4. a
5. a
6. c
7. d
8. a
9. c
10. b

Page 38

1. a
2. c
3. b
4. a
5. d
6. b
7. c
8. c
9. c
10. a

Page 39

1. b
2. a
3. b
4. b
5. c
6. d
7. c
8. a
9. a
10. c

Page 43

1. j
2. e
3. h
4. b
5. g
6. d
7. c
8. a
9. i
10. f
11. Puritans

12. Iroquois
13. indentured servants
14. Quakers
15. Pilgrims
16. Wampanoags
17. lords proprietors
18. Burgesses
19. Parliament
20. Powhatans

Page 45

Native American Words

1. l
2. h
3. i
4. g
5. c
6. j
7. e
8. a
9. f
10. k
11. b
12. d

Indian Place Names

1. Alabama
2. Alaska
3. Arkansas
4. Arizona
5. Connecticut
6. Idaho
7. Illinois
8. Iowa
9. Kansas
10. Kentucky
11. Massachusetts
12. Michigan
13. Minnesota
14. Mississippi
15. Missouri
16. Nebraska
17. New Mexico
18. North Dakota
19. Ohio
20. Oklahoma

Answer Key (cont.)

Page 45 (cont.)
21. South Dakota
22. Tennessee
23. Texas
24. Utah
25. Wisconsin
26. Wyoming

Page 49
1. His mother died of smallpox; his father died in prison.
2. His ship started leaking and had to return to England.
3. She went crazy and drowned herself.
4. Samoset
5. plant the seeds in a mound with three small fish
6. They died of the plague.
7. He sent it to Tom in England.
8. They both wanted Constance Hopkins.
9. He was afraid of Dotey and Leister.
10. John Alden
11. Pilgrims who went to America for religious freedom
12. people who were not of that religion
13. a special Indian like a sachem or wise man
14. He could write.
15. Tom

Page 51
1. a ring in the form of a serpent
2. Robert Carr
3. hunting deer
4. He tried to interest investors in Jamestown.
5. the countess
6. on the orders of Robert Carr
7. It sunk in the Atlantic.

8. to get peace and help from her father
9. Japizaws and his wife
10. John Rolfe
11. Tom Barlow
12. She threw it in the fire.
13. He died on Gates' Gift.
14. Humility
15. She died in England.

Page 54
1. greeted the rising sun
2. 50
3. She laid her head across his breast.
4. the cannon
5. He was adopted into her tribe and was her "brother."
6. He was injured in an explosion.
7. to hold her as a hostage
8. Sir Thomas Dale
9. Japizaw and his wife
10. John Rolfe
11. England
12. how many people were in England, and about the king and queen, John Smith, and the English god
13. illness
14. as a queen and as a curiosity
15. a compass
16. Pocahontas' husband

Page 63

Map 1
1. England
2. tobacco, rice, indigo
3. slaves
4. guns and cloth

Map 2
5. Africa (slave coast)
6. rum, iron
7. slaves
8. sugar and molasses
9. Atlantic Ocean

10. Europe, Africa, North America

Page 64
New England Colonies
1. Connecticut
2. Massachusetts
3. New Hampshire
4. Rhode Island

Middle Colonies
1. Delaware
2. New Jersey
3. New York
4. Pennsylvania

Southern Colonies
1. Georgia
2. Maryland
3. North Carolina
4. South Carolina
5. Virginia

Extension
1. Virginia, 1607
2. Massachusetts, 1620
3. New Hampshire, 1623
4. New York, 1624
5. Connecticut, 1633
6. Maryland, 1634
7. Rhode Island, 1636
8. Delaware, 1638
9. Pennsylvania, 1643
10. North Carolina, 1653
11. New Jersey, 1660
12. South Carolina, 1670
13. Georgia, 1733